WHEELSONG POETRY ANTHOLOGY 3

Edited by

Steve Wheeler
Genevieve Ray
Brandon Adam Haven

First published by
Wheelsong Books
4 Willow Close,
Plymouth PL3 6EY,
United Kingdom

© Wheelsong Poetry, 2023

The right of all featured poets to be identified as the authors of this work have been asserted by them in accordance with the Copyright, Designs and Patents Act of 1988.

Cover photo © Lynda Mary Clifton, 2023
Book design and layout © Steve Wheeler, 2023
First published in 2023

All rights reserved. Except as permitted under current legislation no part of this work may be photocopied, stored in a retrieval system, published, performed in public, adapted, broadcast, transmitted, recorded or reproduced in any form or by any means, without the prior permission of the copyright owners. Any enquiries should be addressed to Wheelsong Books.

Print ISBN: 979-8-86087-765-8

"Genuine poetry can communicate before it is understood."

−T.S. Eliot

FUNDRAISING IN AID OF

Save the Children

Contents

Dedication	Brandon Adam Haven	17
Foreword	The Editors	19
Sunrise	Kehinde Dare	21
Old Bones	Steve Wheeler	21
Spindrift	Gregory Richard Barden	22
Walking on My Tears	Tony Dukeva	23
Adrift No More	Archie Papa	23
Under Cerulean Blue	Amanda Wilson	24
My Silent Slumber	Brandon Adam Haven	25
Being the Unknown Poet	Larry Bracey	25
Look Up	P. G. Holroyd	26
What's at Stake	Joseph Gallagher	27
Disconnected	Jon Wright	28
Reflections	Deanna Repose Oaks	28
The Walk Home	Matt Cording	29
To Dream	Imelda Zapata Garcia	30
Sea of Trees	Gregory Richard Barden	31
I Lost You	Karen Bessette	32
Tio Luis	Manolo Piquero	33
Dark and Lovely	Courtney Glover	34
Cleansing	Tom Cleary	35
Nonsensical Interlude	Hahona Pita Batt	35
The Art of Evening	Iain Strachan	37
Fusion	R. David Fletcher	38
Fountain Plume	Karin J. Hobson	38
Dawn of Silence	Sarah Joy Holden	39
Falling Flowers	James Eaton	39
Those Eyes	Graeme Stokes	40
Manny	Abril Garcia Linn	41
A Backbone Fierce	Torri M. Dobson	42
Shadows	Stasha Strange	42
Sweeping Silhouettes	Charlene Phare	43
Tongue-Tied	Jannetta Lamort	43
Way Back When	Graeme Stokes	44
Disengage	Genevieve Ray	45
The Value of Now	D. Paul McZeal	46

9

I Long to Dance in our Ashes	Mark Heathcote	46
Gift of a Pebble	Phuntsho Wangchuk	47
Binding Story	Pureheart Wolf	48
The Trinity Test	Iain Strachan	48
In One's Beginning	Sheila Grenon	49
In His Shoes	David Grantz	50
The Paint Trickles Down	Cate Buchner	50
Dishonesty	Lisa Combs Otto	51
Ageing Woman	Marie Harris	51
Good News	Rafik Romdhani	52
Much Beauty	Julie Sheldon	52
By Another Name	Archie Papa	53
Only Days	Matt Elmore	53
The Voice	D. A. Simpson	54
Garden of Mind	Selena Ou	55
Take Me to November	Fouzia Sheikh	56
Autumn and Winder	Mark Heathcote	57
To War	Brian Keith	57
Searching for Aurora	Amanda Wilson	58
The Ladder of Life	P. G. Holroyd	59
The Quiet Sea	Neil Mason	59
Sunshine Screams	Steve Wheeler	60
Midnight Lace	Naomi G. Tangonan	60
The Beat of My Heart	Marie Harris	61
The Hate Machine	Larry Bracey	62
I Am	Claire Sutton	63
The Curse	Jon Wright	63
Remembrance	Sarah Joy Holden	64
Café Therapy	Sarah Sansbury	64
In the Midst of the Stormy Sea	Stasha Strange	65
An Unrequited Love	Kelli Walker	66
Afterglow	Sheila Grenon	66
Moon in My Hand	Donna Smith	67
Serengeti	Amanda Wilson	67
Space Stairs	Neil Mason	69
Complicated	Andy Reay	69
Falling Stars	Stasha Strange	70
Dreamt	Fouzia Sheikh	71
Abridgement	Tom Cleary	72
Laundry and Rain	Jack H. DeKnight Jr	73

Shine On	Terry Bridges	73
The Amorist	Brandon Adam Haven	74
Phantom	David Grantz	74
The Ogre Tree	D. R. Parsons	75
Laying Among the Oak	Brandon Adam Haven	76
Community Table	Steven Elliott Borodkin	77
Behind the Willow Tree	Sherry Healy	77
Weeping Orpheus	Madhu Gangopadhyay	79
Mess	D. R. Parsons	80
Green Serene	Graeme Stokes	81
Sunshine Girl	Kelli Walker	82
Don't Judge	Julie Sheldon	83
Vessels	T. M. Warren	84
Bereft of Emotions	Neil Forsyth	85
Poetic Waves	Nan DeNoyer	86
Angel	Jinny Morris	86
Mind Medicine	Cate Buchner	87
A World without Yellow	Joan Audette	87
Catalytic	Markee Reimers	88
Shadows	D. A. Simpson	89
Know This Deer Heart	Jinny Morris	90
I am not Barren	Shafkat Aziz Hajam	91
The Day I Died	Darren B. Rankins	91
Truthfully Yours	Archie Papa	92
Reflections	Jackie Shaffer	92
Whispers	Kieran R. Eldritch	93
Untamed Emotions	Rafik Romdhani	93
Before Morning Twilight	Geoff Edwards	94
London	Tony Dukeva	95
Marble Smasher	Genevieve Ray	96
Dark Times	Minka Leeser	97
Mending	Rhiannon Owens	98
Poetry Never Sleeps	Matthew Elmore	99
How Do You Say Goodbye?	Joan Audette	100
Losing You	Lorna McLaren	101
Sadako – Hiroshima 1955	Sarah Sansbury	101
I Stand/I Cry/I Fly	Shirley Rose	102
Happiness Within	Joel Aparecio Bernasor	102
Lone Figure	Lorna McLaren	103
Afternoon	Jeff Goodman	104

Run	Mike Rose	104
Release the Spirit	Sarfraz Ahmed	105
The Day the Light Went Out	Kirsty Howarth	106
Youth Potion	Sherry Healy	107
Soulmates	Minka Leeser	107
Tranquil Night	Kenneth Wheeler	108
Abyss	Sheri Lemay	108
Wild Beasts	Joe Mendoza	109
My Name is Rage	Pureheart Wolf	110
Remembrance	R. David Fletcher	110
Never Earth	Adookorn Adookorn	111
Low Sky	Anna Obara	111
A Chorus of Sunflowers	Janet Stoyel	112
School Reunion	Genevieve Ray	113
The Girl in the Mirror	Kirsty Howarth	114
Things	Sarah Sansbury	115
I am the Little I am	Matthew Elmore	116
The Passion of the Rose	Patricia Woosley	116
Strange Cacophony	Steve Wheeler	117
Somewhere's Someone	Jeff Goodman	118
Absence	Imelda Z. Garcia	119
Street Punctuation	Geoff Edwards	120
Iridescent	Pritha Lahiri	120
Love	Kirsty Howarth	121
Phoenix from the Dark	Amanda Marchuk	122
Inheritance	T. M. Warren	123
Walk with You	Mike Rose	124
The Kingdom	T. M. Warren	124
Rowdy Day	Adookorn Adookorn	126
R.I.P. No Epitaph Burden	Hahona Pita Batt	127
We All Find Our Peace	Patricia Woosley	129
The Wrath of the Devil	Andy Allen	130
Essential Oil	David Grantz	131
The Irish Wind	Jannetta Lamort	131
Seas and Life	Lorna McLaren	132
Cape Cod in '93	Christopher Black	133
Twelfth Night	Safdar Bhatti	134
Odysseus's Feast from Homer	Ralston Purina	135
Say My Name	Jennifer Torvalson	135
Creativity	Rupa Rao	136

Shower Refrain	Joel Aparecio Bernasor	136
Wrap You in my Arms	Sarfraz Ahmed	137
When Sincerity Meets Serenity	Sarah Wheatley Tillbrook	137
Nightfall	Emediong Asuquo	138
The Wind	Mike Rose	139
Gravel	Imelda Zapata Garcia	140
An Undaunted Woman	Phuntsho Wangchuk	141
Shades of Life	Joel Aparecio Bernasor	142
Solitude	Phuntsho Wangchuk	143
Hopeless	Kieran R. Eldritch	144
A Season of the Gift …	Bernie Martin	144
Damaged Butterfly	Charlene Phare	145
My Forever Senorita	Hahona Pita Batt	145
Our Forgotten Place	Octobias Octobie Mashigo	147
Heavenly Abode	Janet Stoyel	148
Insomniac Poet	Sarfraz Ahmed	149
Delayed Reaction	Charlene Phare	150
Dam the Dawn	Steven Elliott Borodkin	151
Rain	Selena Ou	151
Orbiting Questions	Deepali Parmar	152
I Wish I Could Fly	Richard Harvey	153
In the Dark	Terry Bridges	154
A Home in the Hills	Andy Allen	154
I Remember Bluebells	Christopher Black	155
How to Fulfil Dreams	Shakat Aziz Hajam	155
Summer Storms	Lynne Truslove	156
Touched	Michael Balner	157
Lightning Bugs	Manolo Piquero	158
A South African Sunrise	Bernie Martin	159
Momma's Boy	Jack H. DeKnight Jr	159
A Love Story	Sushma Sharma	160
A Toy	Simon Drake	161
Absence of Belonging	Jennifer Torvalson	162
Untitled	Deepali Parmar	162
DaysNight	Sarah Tillbrook Wheatley	163
Cabbage Patch Agony	Neil Mason	163
The Crescent Moon Bear	Deepali Parmar	164
Where Others saw Chaos…	Patrick Darnell	165
Evening	D. A. Simpson	166
Cuddle Up	Bernie Martin	167

We Are the Invisible	Christopher Black	168
Body, Mind, Spirit	Shirley Rose	169
Grey is Great	Selena Ou	170
Little Funerals	Kelli Walker	171
All Set	Jack H. DeKnight Jr	171
Red Bud	Sherry Healy	172
Turn Around	David Knauss	173
This Day Like Others …	Kwaku Adjei Fobi	174
Summer's Splendor	Manolo Piquero	175
A Song of Light and Dark	D. R. Parsons	176
Panorama of Surprise	Geoff Stockton	177
I Will Change History	Jacob Daniel Laari	178
Gallant Poet	Jannetta Lamort	178
Today	Rhiannon Owens	179
My Darling Boy	Gregory Richard Barden	180
Home	Kwaku Adjei Fobi	182
All I Have	Andy Reay	183
The Stranger	Emediong Asuquo	184
To Wait or Die	Pritha Lahiri	185
Talk to Me	Anna Obara	185
Love's Symphony	S. E. Toner	186
Dig Me a Whole	Gemma Tansey	187
The Trader	Madhu Gangopadhyay	188
The Hazelnut and the …	Iain Strachan	188
It Teases Me	Madhu Gangopadhyay	189
A Restless Soul	Amelia Lynn	190
Whirling Dervishes	Farha Abbasi	191
Between the Trees	Jade Wickens	192
Restless	Jennifer Yorvalson	192
Fragments and Memories	Jacalyn Evone	193
A Stubborn Desire	Kwaku Adjei Fobi	194
The End of the Road	Rafik Romdhani	194
The Rain Lover	Pureheart Wolf	195
A Sonnet to the Setting Sun	Safdar Bhatti	196
Sunset	Kahinde Dare	196

Dedication

This book is dedicated
to the memory
of Tammy Hendrix,
a much loved group member
who this year left us, far too soon.

Saying Goodbye
Brandon Adam Haven

Through sorrow's gate, we bid adieu
As a friend departs; our hearts will rue
A void now lingers, an empty space
With many somber tears upon our face

Yet in our hearts their essence thrives
In gentle memories their spirit survives
Though parted now their presence still near
In whispers soft, we hold them dear

Foreword

Welcome to Wheelsong Anthology 3. This impeccable collection of work by poets from around the world has been curated with the support of members of several Facebook poetry groups including Wheelsong Poetry, Invisible Poets, Poetry UK, Pure Poetry and Safe Haven. Almost 120 poets have poured heart and soul into their individual works, and also for the meaningful cause behind it. As a creative community we stand together in support of the wonderful and essential focus of helping children in need.

This is the third poetry anthology publication by Wheelsong Books in support of Save the Children. As a global charity, Save the Children supports needy children and young people in 115 countries every year. From past anthologies we have been able to raise almost £1500 ($1870) from Amazon sales.

The editorial team has worked fastidiously to deliver a book that stands both in celebration of great poetry and in continuation of the fundraising work accomplished in previous years. Every piece appearing in this book has been rigorously and anonymously peer reviewed.

We believe that immense talent is exhibited on every single page. Whether you submitted your work to this collection or purchased it to read great poetry, you are a part of a worthy cause. We are honoured to present this diverse and high quality collection and we sincerely hope that you enjoy the selection of poems within. Be assured that you have played your part in helping children who are in desperate need.

Steve Wheeler	**Genevieve Ray**	**Brandon Adam Haven**
Poet and Founder	Poet and Playwright	Author of *Into the Grey*
Wheelsong Books		

Sunrise
Kehinde Dare

The bright light
pierced the inky
darkness, torpedoed
the dull cloud and
tornadoed his fireball
into firmament.
He lit the black world
with the illuminating
daylight.

Old Bones
Steve Wheeler

I abhor these old bones.
When they ache. They are prone
To the cold wind that moans.
They feel heavy, like stone.

I loathe these old limbs.
When they fail, they betray.
They are turgid like hymns
On a miserable day.

I despise these old eyes.
They are dim like a lamp
When the wick's compromised
And the taper is damp.

I hate these old hands.
When they shake like a leaf...
But my mind still expands,
And my heart still believes.

Spindrift
Gregory Richard Barden

how proper that I found you for
    my farewell, midst those dunes
        the sands where I did oft' adore
your flesh, daubed by the moon

    o numberless, the softened eves
        those callow hearts would wend
but promises quite often grieve
and swift, would come their end

    to press my kiss upon your eye
dove cheek, soft placed a-palm
I bent to meet your sullen sigh
    so breathed for kindness' calm

    devoutly yours, myself, entire
the draught to draw your wine
    you yet devour'd me, eyes afire
        white-kneed, before your shrine

my blood as passion, let to be
    the sweet sate for your thirst
        a fiery flood you then set free
a seed, consumed and cursed

    o how a laurel placed a-brow
        this man, so chilled and damned
can bring such deed to thus avow
lost love, wrought on the sand

    and tho' I wore a garland, brief
so crowned, for summer's death
our love had withered as a leaf
    'midst autumn's flaming breath.

Walking on My Tears
Tony Dukeva

I was walking on my tears,
I was pelting them with stones,
All the way those toilsome years
I was fighting them alone.

And they felt like thousand spears
Penetrating through my will
And they made me feel so queer
Leaving me in glum bastille.

I am tired of my tears
My soul needs to find repose
Salty sadness is not needed
When the soul expands and grows.

Adrift No More
Archie Papa

While some days I revel in the splendor of it all
time in its distance and love in its fall
in the arms of today with moments at hand
we build memories like castles in sand
And some days I weep as hope would seem lost
sorrow may bargain while tears bear the cost
cast out these moments in shadows of pain
for the sun to dry up like puddles of rain
This is but a feather from the wings of the soul
the clouds of fate leave the wind in control
with life on a journey as time will attest
here on the path where it came to rest

Under Cerulean Blue
Amanda Wilson

Beauty transcending, senses arousing,
sensual, opulence, fragrance of you.
Cascading red curls, tousled, alluring,
tempting, enchanting, beguiling the view.
Mirrors to your soul, your eyes of sky blue.
Jasmine and orchids the garlands you wear,
draped around your nape, entwined in your hair.

Sea-scented aura, a whispering breeze,
crystal clear waters and golden white sands.
Romantic setting, memories to please,
a forest backdrop for luxe wedding plans.
Summer love feelings in far distant lands.
Petals from blossoms enhancing the view,
vows exchanged under cerulean blue.

Beneath a pink canopy at twilight,
encircled palm trees of emerald green,
ceremony enchanting, bride in white,
red plaited tresses, beautiful; serene.
A vision of splendour, donned like a queen.
A flower garland attached to your veil,
the Mockingbird sings like the Nightingale.

The first 'star' Venus appears at sunset,
love aisle bathes in a vision of light.
Beauty surreal, sunset silhouette,
coral reef beneath unseen in moonlight.
Voile arch and vows declared in the spotlight.
Almond eyes shine a reflection I see,
two brides in love in blissful harmony.

Blessing stone tradition, wishes and prayers,
shoreline guests gather a silent wish penned.
An ocean of love, stones thrown to declare,
engraved special thoughts good wishes extend.
Thankful and grateful our friends could attend.
A Mockingbird still sings for me and for you,
beneath moonlit skies of *cerulean blue*.

My Silent Slumber
Brandon Adam Haven

I softly slumber in silent sempiternity
Amidst the anguish of quietude, I languish
Entombed beneath the soil's solemn nourish
An empty respite beckons, a melancholic flourish
Where shadows commune with stillness brim
In somnolent repose, ensconced in sin
With empty solace, enshrouded in flame
Within the hallowed depths weeping disdain
Decaying my carcass, weak with no brawn
In my silent slumber, mirroring eternity's dawn

Being the Unknown Poet
Larry Bracey

I'm offering you a taste,
Of a fruit I'd never bitten,
Putting myself out there,
In every word I've written,
Becoming my characters,
To see where the story will go,
Being inspired by the likes,
Of Shakespeare, and Marlowe,
Using personal experience,
And all the things I've seen,
Expressing how I feel,
So the lyrics are crisp and clean,
Wanting you to understand it,
While tugging at your heart,
Stories that keep you reading,
Even when they tear you apart,
Because somehow we are connected,
We feel what others feel,
There's something about empathy,
That makes them all seem real.

Look Up
P. G. Holroyd

Look up…
…at every rain-drenched cloud,
with lightning bright and thunder loud,
the wrath of nature at her worst
she orders all the clouds to burst
The weakest race we run for cover
terrified of Nature's mother
as if we'd done her wrong somehow
and so she wants to kill us now
Look up…
…into the deep blue skies
where blazing sun attacks your eyes
and tries to burn your tender skin,
again we have to hide within
The faded moon will blow a kiss
behind the endless blue abyss,
a reminder that our whole life's worth
is but a blink to Mother Earth
Look up…
…and see the darkest night,
a billion stars are shining bright,
our curiosity running rife imagining all
kinds of life
If we could wave a magic wand
and reach another world beyond
perhaps we'd see someone like you
looking up into the blue
Look up…
…and see the world around
with all its wonders to be found,
mountains, rivers, giant trees, rolling
hills and raging seas
All the plants and living souls
acting out their given roles,
we're nothing but a tiny crease in
Mother Nature's masterpiece

What's at Stake
Joseph Gallagher

Before Shakespeare invented the anti-hero
Before DaVinci discovered the dark side of the moon
Before the star's eyelids were wrapped in silk
Because their beauty was too much to bear...
That's when the soul whispers for you to draw near
And sings if you were any more stunning,
Surely I would be blinded, surely my spirit would break—
I answered, let my heart be what's at stake.

I never claimed darkness was my father
Or that the road I walked on was called despair.
I may be foolish for believing the wind remembers
Our sorrows, and carries them clean towards the sea...
They rise, like an aroma of roses to nimbus clouds of rain,
He winds wish to wash us fresh of our reoccurring pain.
Our memories hold them down beneath a depthless lake—
I must remember to let my heart be what's at stake.

I saw a dancer in red high heels leap skyward
On a moon strewn beach in Old Orchard Maine.
She seemed to levitate just above the Boardwalk,
In that instant I imagined the concept of the soul
Caught between time and space, here and now
Between body and blood and whatever comes next,
Like a dream of a place where the soul comes to sleep...
And if it dies before I wake—
Let my heart be what's at stake.

And if our silence or our prayers cut us loose
Suspended in time, let us go falling from our doubts
Like high-wire acrobats without a net,
Our arches curved, our spines like smoke...
Ready, if not eager to break from all we grieve
Prepared like ghosts to disappear, to take our leave.
Our lives are what we think, do, feel and make—
Let our hearts be what's at stake.

Disconnected
Jon Wright

Blue screens on faces dancing
As frantic fingers prancing
Social media darkening skies
As real interaction dies
Seeing all we know through phone screen
Nothing in real life seen

A thirst for comments and likes
No more summer days on bikes
No truth, no reality on display
Doctored photos, fake friends every day
In a rush to be liked, to maintain our youth
For going everything, even the truth
No more connection, we are all disconnected

Reflections
Deanna Repose Oaks

Chanting Mirror Mirror on the Wall
Never revealed beauty at all
Reflections warped within the glass
By all the sins of the past
Blocked the beauty I sought to seek
Within the glass so shiny and sleek
I touch the surface hoping to fall through
Into a world where love rules true
But all I feel is my glance
That bounces back at every chance
I want to hear the glass as it breaks
But fear the years that it takes
The sins are echoing oh so loud
They are really starting to crowd
I'm torn with wanting my mirror down
Because I still want to see my crown

The Walk Home
Matt Cording

Hazy lamp posts assist my walk through a speckled yellow glow
The sounds of falling raindrops up and down these sodden roads
The deadened sound of footsteps no trace from whence they came
No proof of where and when I joined this dampened walking game

Others walking by, some with a quickened pace
Mostly with head held down so as not to show their face
So many reasons to account for that anonymity being one
Although getting rain down your collar really isn't much fun

It's slowed for now, although persistent drops still falling
Off the leaves and on to cars as they drive by crawling
A summers rain creates a mist hovering in the night
Shadowy figures appear and disappear, it seems a trick of light

Overflowing gutters leading to splashes all around
Creating a tinkling crashing sound as those splashes
Hit a discarded carrier bag lying upon the ground
That tap tap tapping it's such a distinctive sound

The mist still present leaving swirls as I am walking through
They drift behind me down the road looping as they do
Each patch catching shades of light even when I'm slow
Leaving strange reflections in the puddles as I go

Walking in the rain at night, are you a lover or a hater,
I feel if you're walking and in love there's almost nothing greater
It feels as though each drop is caressing you as you walk
Still feeling the glow inside me from when I last heard you talk

A fox appears just trotting, it seems not a care in the night
No umbrella needed for him as he nonchalantly trots on by
Up the rain it picks again as if to say go home
No time for dilly dallying although still time to look at pics
Of you my love, I'd taken on my phone.

Through the door and warm towels are the order of the day
My phone goes ding; it's as if you were with me all the way
You laugh at my drenching although for me inside I feel
Each drop each drip was you proving your love as solid
As solid as love can sometimes feel.

To Dream
Imelda Zapata Garcia

the curtains fall to shroud the call
which tugs incessantly
as dreams stall
late in darkened slumber
as I await and count the number
of hours it takes, to slow escape
a drugging nudging
in thunderous squall

naught a cloud up in the ether
no storm brewing, lightning, neither
yet the clamoring of threat
upon a dreary weary nape
feeds pervasive thoughts
I'd soon forget

wakefulness hangs heavy to the dawn
dreaming, fleeting glances from then on
clapping of a throbbing pounding drawn
creating colored circles of a fawn
around the eyes or there upon

a constant droning taps on moments
honing in on mindless snaps
crowding sleepless stretch
of hands in periodic tocks
leaving me a hopeless wretch

Sea of Trees
Gregory Richard Barden

jade canopy
waving while it
whispers
the lush secret, compelled
delicious word
of myriad words
casting shadowed
merriment at a woven
briar carpet

colored strings, winding... waiting

tangled labyrinth,
so deep and
dark that dew still clings
at mid-day,
leafy tresses tickling azure,
sopping sun
like thirst—bright and
warm above
straight trunks like steady
soldiers

fingery tendrils
burrow deep to find purchase
 —ruddy earth, cool as
rime, rich with
rooty rot—nature's marrow
to breathe the
branches

Fuji's frilly garden skirt

listen, tender...
soft now, the hush
of mys'tries—
this forest bides all, yet

stars still glisten its black heart—
desire, a mossy coat ...
dour... waiting

hear the voice, low,
the breath of breaths, murmuring—
it begs, come...
in a thousand gentle
lullabies, with
the language of the ages
and the ends—

voice sweet as death

it calls to
the misty meandering,
one dire dalliance—
grandest adventure of all—
the dazzling dream
that *never*
wakes.

I lost You
Karen Bessette

I lost you that day in the rain.
I went home and
looked out the window
for you to come back,
but only the sparrows
spoke in the trees.
I listened for a while,
restless and confused
waiting for the rain to stop,
and my heart to understand
why love sometimes leaves.

Tio Luis
Manolo Piquero

Remember when you used to take us to the park
behind the big apartment building where we all lived?
The Bronx was a big scary place when you're 10,
but not when I was with you, I always felt safe.
I thought you were so cool with your shades
and a cigarette always hanging from your lips.
Unshaven most of the time and wearing an army jacket,
Starsky and Hutch couldn't hold a match to you.
We'd sit on the stoop at Abuelita's after dark,
especially in the summer, when it was too hot to stay inside.
Sometimes you let me sneak into your sister's room and
You'd let me play with all her stuff on her dresser.

I'd go into your room and look at all your drawings;
you started taking up painting that year
and your pastoral scenes mesmerised me.
You never minded when I'd flip through all your vinyl albums
and asked you who these artists were on the covers.
One day, you stopped coming around.
Mom told me you were sick and couldn't come.
More days pass and Mom said let's go,
we were going to see you in Bellevue.
Words started coming up in conversations,
'Sick', 'addiction', 'Heroin'.
You were in bed and only looked at the ceiling.
I was 10, what was I to know how bad you had it.

That was the last time I ever saw you.
Weeks later, my mother said to me that you died,
She explained as best she could to a 10 year old,
while fighting back her own tears,
that you were hit by a car, and died right there.
Later as Mom talked to her sisters in the living room,
they never knew, but I heard what they said that day.
They said you were so high when it happened,
you never saw the car coming.
My mother lost her baby brother that day,

I lost an uncle, my role model, my friend,
the big brother I always wanted and never had.
I imagine you telling God,
"Hey God, give that kid a break.
He's trying hard don't you see.

He didn't have a chance to grow up,
with me to show him what's what."
You know, I never got to say goodbye to you,
and I guess I just wanted to tell you
one more thing up there in Heaven,
"I forgive you."
Forgive you for what, you're asking me?
I forgive you for being a selfish uncle, brother and son.
I forgive you for putting mi Madre, tus hermanas, y tu madre
through all that pain, for just one more hit.
Just one more high.

I forgive you for not letting me grow up
with an amazing uncle whom I wanted to be exactly like.
I forgive you for not being there when I need someone to talk to
about girls, music, my art, my life.
I forgive you Tio.

Dark and Lovely
Courtney Glover

I'm ardently in love with all things dark and lovely
Filled with eccentric curiosities sublime and behovely

An admirer of curious curios and objet d'art
A devotee of all things esoteric and macabre
An enamored soul of all things odd and aberrant
For I am a lover of all things dark,
lovely and frighteningly errant

Cleansing
Tom Cleary

Silence sashays down cold alleyways
Her taffeta gown cleansing the air
ridding it of recondite
murmurs in the night.

Nonsensical Interlude
Hahona Pita Batt

A delirium dosed
differential mind
primes cerebral
delinquent exhalations

Flatulent Bohemians
bumfuzzle troglodytes
in discombobulated
vociferous articulate...
burgeoning rainbow
expletive facetious diatribe

Aphrodite's sumptuous bosom
silhouettes man's primal gloats
liquidating noob egos
in mercurial placate

Neath blasé moistened
portion terse
pinion legs seize
in rusted grind
rendering carnal duels
to pastel toned chaste

Notions of Tequila sozzled
tumbleweed players

donning Sombreros...
blottoed & besotted in
100 proof
cactus brine

Tangential minds
fester in
primordial snooze...
top shelf notions
ameliorate sobriety

Tepid player's
pay homage
to rambunctious
proteus prosperous
poet's purging
Flora's seed

Neath boughs & bouquets
a bespoke
vignette life
falters in
illogical boolean
disarray

Tired beyond calamity
this enervated
portly gargoyle
seminally yields

Supplication of
quixotic poetical bones
a timely sabbatical
ebbing evermore...
& gladly lost
upon an Empyreal sea
of sempiternity.

The Art of Evening
Iain Strachan

Thus wends the redness in the sunlight's fall.
A warming colour as the evening cools
portends the exit of our star, its crawl
below the line, painting with darker tools.

A warming colour as the evening cools
collapsing down to richer, deeper shades
below the line painting with darker tools,
a wilder palette blooms as daylight fades.

Collapsing down to richer, deeper shades
with scattered rays from atmospheric dust,
a wilder palette blooms as daylight fades,
till darkness comes as darkness always must.

With scattered rays from atmospheric dust
the optics conjures up an artist's paint
till darkness comes as darkness always must,
the gloaming gliding, slowly growing faint.

The optics conjures up an artist's paint,
a brush of colour in the waning sky
the gloaming gliding slowly growing faint,
unveiling pointillistic stars on high.

A brush of colour in the waning sky
portends the exit of our star, its crawl,
unveiling pointillistic stars on high.
Thus wends the redness in the sunlight's fall.

Fusion
R. David Fletcher

Dreams of dolls and atom bombs,
Awash in pastel mushroom clouds,
Market hype and media songs,
Delirium of the dazzled crowds.

Fountain Plume
Karin J. Hobson

Enigma found betwixt the lines
Third eye dances in moonlight
Vellum paper kisses feather,
Silent whispers release tether.

Blots of magick or misty stardust
Line is straight or perhaps not there;
Is it a man or be he a king;
And, what of the next line, is she queen?

If, put to paper or of foot to go
You are director to take or forgo;
Onward to China to view Great Wall
Or, to Heaven's notable Library Hall?

Worries banished or brought to bear
Even vows like 'I do solemnly swear'
Are cast in black to attack white
Candle burning on thru the nite

Eos unleashes window blinds
Cock crows announcing time,
Tis the hour of unfeigned gloom
Laying down mine fountain plume.

Dawn of Silence
Sarah Joy Holden

Silence is the dawn
Standing all alone
Glistening on the horizon
Veiled by a gentle breeze

Silence is the dawn
Upon the hills and valleys
Nature draws her breath
With mist upon her fields

Silence is the dawn
Earth turns on its axis
Light and dark rotation
Broken by morning larks

Silence is the dawn
That earth slowly awakens
Upon God's amazing creation
As dawn's silence now breaks.

Falling Flowers
James Eaton

Flowers fall through empty space,
Faded petals, card and face.
How we met and where we stayed,
Where the seaside house displayed,
Pink carnations round the door,
Petals scattered on the floor.
Holding hands along the beach,
Everything so out of reach.
Evening strolls through empty streets,
Waves of silence, no one greets,
Seagulls calling from the sea,
Lonely as both you and me.

Those Eyes
Graeme Stokes

Where did you get, where did you get those eyes?
They're sure to disarm, with their dreamy charm,
from heaven?
I can only surmise
They break down the walls of my fragile defence
Brick by brick, falls my patent pretence
Suddenly the world makes perfect sense
I'm under their spell, let the healing commence
From those eyes my love, those eyes!
Where did you get, where did you get those eyes?
In my hour of need, when I'm stranded at sea,
they're my boat that won't capsize!
From my autumnal malaise, they're sweeping a clearing
A seamless transition, to a sun that's searing
From my empty heart, clouds are disappearing
With hope renewed, I'm now persevering
Because of those eyes, my love, those eyes!
Where did you get, where did you get those eyes?
They're my compass to guide me, they subtly ride me,
to the place I fantasise!
From their treasure trove of secret stashes
A light reprimand, from luxurious lashes
In this celestial moment, my spirit detaches
As their stirring flame, smoulders and flashes
Those eyes at me, my love, those eyes!
Where did you get, where did you get those eyes?
It wasn't by chance, I fell into this trance,
as they sparkle and mesmerise
As they pluck at my heartstrings,
I'm compelled to endeavour
To dance to their tune, drifting light as a feather
On this moonlit lake I'll be floating forever
In your eyes, my love, your eyes!

Manny
Abril Garcia Linn

I see you in the amber glow of the city lights at night
I hear you in the rhythm
of San Anto music, raw and rasquache
I smell you in the steamy corn tortillas
of the westside Molino
I feel you in the warm wind of
Woodlawn lake on a sunny day
I see you in the smile of la chula chicana
dancing polkas with her man at the pulga
I hear you in the rapid pulse of San Anto streets
flowing with life
I smell you in the alcohol soaked sweat of a musician
after a late night gig
I feel you in the clear spring fed water
of Paradise Canyon, cooling my toes

I see you in the rough brown skin
of that suave pachuco in the back of the bar
I hear you in the tap tap tap of feet moving
to conjunto grooves at Rosedale Park
I smell you in the aftershave of the viejito smoking
a Marlboro on his front porch
I feel you in the humid heat and searing
burn of the South Texas summer sun

I see you in the vibrant colors
and dazzling images of San Anto Westside murals
I hear you in the gritos of los necios at the Spurs games
I smell you in the sizzle of burning meat
at the backyard barbeque
I feel you in the embrace of a beloved friend
that has been long missed

You never left
You transformed into everything
that you ever loved.

A Backbone Fierce
Torri M. Dobson

Sometimes I fear writing,
Words spilling from my eyes
I don't want to lose my feelings
of regret, pain, and guilt
They are all I seem to know
I have lost enough already
But I finally have the courage
To let peace in.
Sometimes, I am the poet.
Sometimes, I am the poem.
Sometimes, I am the page.

Shadows
Stasha Strange

In shadows deep, where anger grows,
A tale of vengeance fiercely flows.
No mercy held, no heart to spare,
Desire for revenge fuels the air.
Limb from limb, the tearing starts,
A reckoning for wounded hearts.
No thought of consequence or cost,
In pursuit of what is truly lost.
But heed this warning, darkened soul,
Vengeance exacts its heavy toll.
A cycle spun, a spiral spun,
A bitter end when all is done.
The shadow's fate, a lonely one,
Forgotten in the setting sun.
Yet ask yourself, what have you won,
When all is said and vengeance done?

Sweeping Silhouettes
Charlene Phare

Sweeping silhouettes through the night
Drawing rainbow colours away
Shadows lurking, bewildered sight
Plunged into darkness of dismay
Rainbow colours drifted away
Stillness of time dampens the air

Lingered shadows, causing affray
Atmospherics laying bare
Time frozen releasing despair
Pausing the past in our clutches
Toxins expelled into mid-air
Kissing surfaces it touches
Past safely paused in our clutches
We're never letting it out of sight
Beauty from within, it touches
Sweeping silhouettes from our nights

Tongue-Tied
Jannetta Lamort

"Six tall, slick, slim sycamore trees."
Say that three times,
and again, and once more."
Teeth and tongue sticking together—
My mother made me master this meter
"Stop, stop, stop—now, say it right."
Slippery, sliding, syllables, and I struggle—
Wondering if my message
was worth all this trouble.

Way Back When
Graeme Stokes

Back in the day, he still remembers when
The days seemed superfluous, the years were his friends
They were straightforward and upright, simple and clear
Neighbour knew neighbour, the streets held no fear
He was wholesome and strong, he held the advantage
Now he sits weak and frail, from his peripheral vantage
His pockets were full, on the good times he spent
But this is now, and that was then!
It's all knick-knacks and apps, and plastic that governs
For his pounds, shillings and pence,
no one gives a tuppence!
Through watery eyes, that dart and peruse
He beholds the fresh feet, to fill his old shoes
As the youth leaps the stairs, in twos at a time
'Good luck son!' he whispers, and prays he'll do fine
He took life in his stride, way back when
But this is now, and that was then!
He tries to keep up, to stay in the loop
But it's all so damn fast, for a hunch and a stoop
The bewildering attire, and the alien phrases
He has not the words, for these modern day ladies!
He was the Brillcream pin up, the creme de la creme!
But this is now, and that was then!
His lines tell of tales, through trails nigh complete
Like an ordnance survey, with a map obsolete
He's now rigid of limb, with unbending hips
His head just won't settle, like his wintery wisps
On grey days he ponders, if he really should stay?
Since his to have and to hold, was taken away!
Riding on sunsets, tomorrow's without end
But this is now, and that was then!

Disengage
Genevieve Ray

We are free
To disengage
Turning into nothing
Our hand prints
Washed by time
Clean of each other
Empty of lost palms

We are free
To disengage
Distant whistles
Latent notions
Fresh Spring courtships
Clean-slate passions
New reckonings

We are free
To disengage
The chance encounter
May lead to a nod
A smile for kindness
Side-step dance
Racing to new futures
More pressing responsibilities

We are free
And slowly disengage

Forgetting lawn trees
Speckled shadows
Any lingering feelings
In slow sadness
The end of a friendship

The Value of Now
D. Paul McZeal

As the world turns and no one knows,
What the times of the future really hold,
And where distant histories are left behind,
In a far-distant past where it's hard to find,
The many dreams you had of pie in the sky,
That withered away into a hazy by and by,
And though you did your best to make things work,
You found out, in the end, a mindful kind of hurt,
Then you paused to uncover the courage to start again,
With more zeal and vigor than when you first began,
To try and make amends for all the mistakes,
You made for yourself and came to hate,
Then you found out as time moved on,
You could never go back to fix the right or wrongs,
Nor the desires and plans that lay thick in your past,
That never came forth or they failed to last,
But today you can seize from where you've come,
To see and embrace a life that is second to none,
Still looking forward in delight and clinging to how
Your destiny is always attached to the value of Now!

I Long to Dance in our Ashes
Mark Heathcote

If every drop has been-tasted
—and seasoned with love.

Not even the bones of love
the perspiration-of-passion is wasted.

Not one more drop on my lips,
could quench the fires we've ignited.

I long to dance in our ashes,
bathe in the afterglow of our cinders.

Gift of a Pebble
Phuntsho Wangchuk

To you, to others, to the world entire,
It's just a pebble, a worthless pebble;
An extraneous and a valueless stone
Which at measure of time can be
Easily fetched and instantly forgotten.
But for me it's not just a pebble mere;
There are much more things enshrined
Within it: most joyous moment of life:
The cream of my childhood is etched
And baked within this black, bare body.
Our hearts saw each before our eyes
And knew faster than our conscience;
As the minutes matured into our days,
Strangeness grew into a love sublime
And engirdled our souls into one bond.
Under the command of the heaven,
Herding the cattle in the village outskirts;
(She herded for her family, I for mine)
But with one common in us always:
Two souls blended like tears in a fire.
We'd meet every morn with our cattle
And play games of Toss and Catch stones,
Trading our thoughts, mixing our laughter
Like our cattle mingled afield to graze,
Until the day retired into its dusty dusk.
Love and promises ruled those days
And the heaven fell down to the earth;
Wrapped in her love, sealed by promises;
She gifted me a pebble on one such day
And thence she's never seen, never heard.
At this age, I still receive many such gifts:
Gifts on my birthdays, gifts for successes;
Gifts of various types and varied prices;
Yet they hardly can reach my heart deep
For my heart's sealed by this little pebble.

Binding Story
Pureheart Wolf

You absorbed me in your story
And slowly etched into my brain
You captured my monochrome essence
And beckoned me to play.

Now we meet between the pages
Only words without the sound.
Bonded within a library book
In the centre of my town.

The Trinity Test
Iain Strachan

To break unholy atoms, blow apart:
Not God, but man was bending nature's force
A fission chain-reaction at its heart,
Refiner's fire was wrought to end all wars.

The tree of knowledge bore its tainting fruit:
Plutonium—a sphere of grapefruit size
With neutrons, spreading virus-like to shoot
The kilotons to Hell—satanic prize!

As he beheld the blind blaspheming cloud
A revelation filled the scorching flames
The Hindu scripture spoke as if aloud
Battered his heart, declaimed these fearful names—

O World-Destroyer, unbecoming Death!
O guilt to burn him till his final breath!

In One's Beginning
Sheila Grenon

I'll build you a home in the meadow, he said...

Generations changing all over
Welcoming moments before
our eyes seeing that *beginning*,
the North set nought, all not quite figured out

Starting with how the *west* was won
By tyranny, disgrace, determination and grit
We will win this rat-race I must admit

Time changes people
Time changes life
Time changes earth
Time changes hearts

The Alamo, fights and pain in futility
Precious living life walked trails unity
As the rest followed nearer
Determination sought pain clearer

Fighting the good fight
Keeping all intentions in sight
Loving friendships wrought
Existence of homes bought

Over the horizon we see...
Miracles calling out to you and me
Generational pulls form distinctively
Horses neigh in positivity.

In His Shoes
David Grantz

They had always lived to travel,
she, a diamond on his arm.
When they'd stepped out
to isles or mountains,
their smiles entranced the world.
They regaled all whom they'd encountered,
whether homeward or afar.
Together, they'd made harmony
that interlaced their roving stars,
as they chased their common moon.
Those precious sojourns had framed their love
and sent them back to years flown by;
then chilly winds had interposed
to take him from her and invoke
the oath that they had sworn.
As evening deepened into purples,
she poured again her wine
and his—house red, unbranded.
Tomorrow, Athens, next day, Delphi,
then their moon above Olympus,
shared with strangers in his shoes.

The Paint Trickles Down
Cate Buchner

The paint trickles down
Like tears on an angel's face
But why so sad
The air breathes a sigh of summer relief

The dusty dry earth cracks
Letting us view the mystery which lies
beneath the surface
And we run scared of knowing.

Dishonesty
Lisa Combs Otto

She seemed to be drawn
to the incurable dishonesty
that fell effortlessly from their lips.
Those delicious lips that brought about
unreasonable amounts of pure joy.
She lived in the duality of it.
Perpetually disoriented.

Ageing Woman
Marie Harris

Timeless beauty
Etched into the lines of age upon her face
A plateau of defined beauty
Seen in the depths of her eyes
A settled smile of confidence worn
Years have treated her kindly
She is at peace with her life
Love has graced her frame
Laughter has added a dimensional
Elegance in fine lines adorning
A silken sheen shines in her greying hair
Composed and in tune with the music
Alive in her soul
In her smile the mystery of woman
There contained
She is tenderness in a steel backbone
Through the flames of life
A Phoenix rising
Resilient and strong
Weathering the storms through the years
A wife, mother, aunt, sister, daughter
A woman in the glory days of
A balanced, well lived life

Good News
Rafik Romdhani

She drowned me in the long night of her arms
and wept like a cloud stuck in love's barbed wire.
We closed our eyes like two swallows
to see the horizon within.
All standing we slept, never caring
about the wind which took our shoes off
to fill them with good news, with infinite paths,
with stories now turned into sand.
She drowned me like a deluge of emotions,
a crazy current sepulchring the bones
and moans of a shivering Phlebas.

Much Beauty
Julie Sheldon

A calm winter walk as the sun sets
The birds sing a sweet lullaby
A beautiful tune to welcome the moon
As the sun waves her nightly goodbye

The clouds glow like fiery embers
Each moment brings new shades to love
A glorious sight prepares for the night
As the bright stars appear up above

The world has much beauty to offer
You just have to look for the signs
So listen and see, it's all there for free
You just need your ears and your eyes

By Another Name
Archie Papa

Life will form a curving path
on lines of time we endure
making fate the aftermath
and truth the honest allure
Heartbeats keep a sacred pace
time, the expression of light
love will be the only grace
ending the battles we fight
Life and time are bonded true
by strides and steps we take
those we lose or misconstrue
our hearts may not forsake
Moments lost and those well spent
their brilliance just the same
all received as heaven sent
was love by another name

only days
Matthew Elmore

what are these to be but only days?
to kiss to dream to slip away
for a moment in time, never to stay
what are these to be but only days?
what is life to be but only this?
to share to love to leave to miss
successful failure; oh wretched bliss!
what is life to be but only this?
what more to have but more to lose
to pay the toll with years as dues
the sun shall fall, then slowly fade
what are these to be, but only days?

The Voice
D. A. Simpson

The voice that is heard a-blowing
among the trees of the forest
Across lakes and oceans and through hamlets a many

The voice that whispers
in the quiet of shadows on a summer's day

The voice that echoes amid valleys
And rises o'er the world's loftiest peaks
skimming their snow-capped heights

The voice that sings
among meadows of green
and golden deserts covering empty 'scapes

Is the voice that answers the cry of an orphan
The voice that soothes the widow
and mends a spirit broken from grieving

It is the voice that breathes healing into a wound

It is the voice which soothes
the weary bones of those who toil
and directs those who travel

It is the voice of the one
who settles the seas and skies at night
and rouses them anew at dawn

Garden of Mind
Selena Ou

Push worry into a metal box,
and anxiety into another one and
anguish, sadness, inquests…
put a lock on each of them, make it tight!

The garden of mind at night
should now be calm and quiet,
as silk in the air and
mist on the lakes or in the deep forests.

I must have been cursed
before embarking Noah's Ark.
The Devil boarded with me,
as life did not turn to paradise.
Harsh childhood paved into adult paths and
sweet dreams often become nightmares.

Is it true that kindness and niceness
are the tokens of the deficient?
Like smooth pebbles, from years' endurance
surviving in a torrent,
and bamboo bending humbly to stand up
after thunder and storm.

The realisation hurts.

Yet the river keeps running,
Rain goes and sun does come, sometimes.

When the darkness drops,
I hope my garden of mind will be free of battle,
calm and quiet.

Take Me to November
Fouzia Sheikh

They say it's the month of sadness.
Where all old sad memories recalled
With faint dry sound of wind
Like footsteps of passing ghosts.
Pale moon painted all red,
Dancing crows and thunder
Black spells to see the dead.
Take me to November.
When colours melt,
Just as they fall
Stripping down to shadows.
Not all months behave like you.
So dull and dark are November twilights,
The lazy mist high up and everything curled.
And the nights are getting cold,
They've put shawls of fog around them,
See what if the air should grow so dimly white.
That we would lose our way along the paths.
Made by walls of moving mist receding,
The more we follow....
What a silver night.
Take me to November
November comes and goes so dark,
wet and gloomy.
Where the nostalgia and departure
separated your shadow.

Autumn and Winter
Mark Heathcote

As for spring and summer
I can wake a hummingbird in you
make an eagle hover to devour you
as for autumn and winter
in her final grip, their icy moans.

I can call a vulture to pick your bones
make you, my robin redbreast.
Strip your feathers to line my soul's nest.
And as for all the rest; let-eternity
know that I've been devoutly blest.

To War
Brian Keith

Who are we but martyrs,
To the dollar that we lay,
A government that would sacrifice,
The public in this way,
To war our soldiers will journey,
To die on foreign land,
To kill the people from other places,
Sent there by a protected man,
Standing on his mighty lectern,
To preach of life and sacrifice,
To speak of pride and waving flags,
Behind his back a sharpen knife,
Freedom has a mighty cost,
A fight that will never end,
Our soldiers are to be honored,
Though our government is not a friend.

Searching for Aurora
Amanda Wilson

Mother earth's flawless, light boreal wild
o'er Scandia skies, ribbons stream and dance.
Multi-coloured, a midnight's canvas styled,
searching for aurora, a transient glance.
Divine illumes, celestial en-trance.
A perfect arc on dark drift-less nights,
ether's spiritual smile, the northern lights.

Crystal stars shine in a darkened ink sky,
'neath heaven ships sail, ayond polar seas.
Aurora chariot race in the mind's eye,
glaciated spectrum of colour tease.
Luminous, radiance in arctic freeze.
Goddess of dawn and God of north wind seen
dancing away in a nightclub of green.

The 'Fire fox' lights the snowy arctic fells,
myths and legends, Finnish folklore's ideal.
Through pine forests branches lustre bespells,
the chromatic phenomenon; Surreal!
Double aura photo secrets reveal.
For hunters chasing the aurora's trail,
the beauty, the veil, the night's holy grail.

Polar prism of joy, magic night convey,
stars bathe in a kaleidoscope of dreams.
Glowing, intense, sensorial display,
reaching skyward to the upper extremes.
Pinks, red and purples, rainbow colour schemes.
The ink darkened sky now blue breaks the morn,
blessed Aurora to this your new dawn.

The Ladder of Life
P. G. Holroyd

I'm past the halfway mark as I climb towards the dark
never knowing when my journey's going to end;
glancing down the rungs I've passed feels like
I climbed it way too fast
but the only choice I have now is ascend

It only makes me sadder that I can't descend the ladder
unless I lose my grip and plummet down,
seeing all my life flash by in the blinking of an eye
before my steps all crumble back into the ground

On my climb I often find lots more ladders intertwined,
some stay with me and others drift apart,
occasionally they fall or they never climb at all,
a broken ladder means a broken heart

So I cling for dear life through the laughter and the strife
and keep my footing firmly on the rungs,
one step at a time as I make the steady climb
as long as there's still air inside my lungs

My ending might be soon or I could climb to the moon,
nobody knows the moment they will fall
unless they hit a slump and decide they'd rather jump,
I hope that feeling never comes to call

The Quiet Sea
Neil Mason

No whisper or words of anger did I hear
The quiet sea did not make a sound
Just a vast blue calmness
It only gave me a wave

Sunshine Screams
Steve Wheeler

Sunshine screams its mischievous reforms
Guitar strings fold the motion of the waves
Love pirouettes the clouds of dying storms
Vicious gossip seeps from fresh dug graves

Across the airwaves of this wanton sphere
We try to catch the thunder, but we fail
Our hearts grow colder in this atmosphere
Our fears like tears hang from the nail

Trapped inside those whimsied escapades
Chimera cameras capture potent threats
The mantra is repeated there in spades
and before you ask, we haven't got there yet

Unseen, the beings preen on dancing plains
the stains of their existence are their melody
A tune direct injects into my vectored veins
Arcane refrains contain cacophony.

I heard the shape-shift bird below me shout
It bellowed through a rainbow-hued device
A murmur came to mind that gave no doubt
That there can never be a compromise

Midnight Lace
Naomi G. Tangonan

midnight lace
a spider's web
shines in the dark

The Beat of My Heart
Marie Harris

The past beats inside me like a second heart
Long ago memories that flood my dreams
Chasing a remembered happiness
Shining with a delicate glowing ember

Like a fragile flower with a forever bloom
A remembered fragrance
Permeates my senses from time to time

On a fragmented tour of yesterday
In shades of saffron and gentle blues

A delicate timbre that softly thuds
Against the walls of my emptiness

Scattered remnants blown about by winds of change
Hellos, goodbyes
Life flourishing
Life succumbing
To the inevitable
Process of ageing

Golden days filled with echoing peals of laughter
Amidst a sudden onslaught of tears
Shedding the layer of years
Among the dying roses

Perceptions dimmed
Possibilities waning
Life is tenacious, holding on
Not wanting to dive into
The ocean of forgetfulness
To wash ashore
In the purple stain of twilight's dusk
A stranger to myself

A timid little beat
Repeats and repeats
Your time is not yet complete

The Hate Machine
Larry Bracey

My mother spoke of the hate machine,
And the evil that men do,
How history always repeats itself,
Which I've seen a time or two,
We dust off the hate machine,
And Grease up the gears,
Hoping it feeds into paranoia,
Awakening your fears,
An eye for an eye,
Fuelling this machine of hate,
Refusing to sit together,
Or Let alone debate,
Generations of people,
Being taught to hate,
Based on religion,
and reasons they can't relate,
The innocence of youth,

Tainted by the ignorance of men,
Being led into a battle,
Yet once again,
Violence overcomes us,
Tension thick in the air,
Misguided actions
Leaving death everywhere,
Once the line is crossed,
There is no turning back,
People rarely forgive,
The moment you attack ,
The innocence of youth,
Tainted by the ignorance of men,
Being led into a battle,
Yet once again.

I Am
Claire Sutton

I am the autumn leaves that fall
I am the trees that stand so tall
I am the stars twinkling at night
I am the sunshine, I am the light
I am the winter chill that blows
I am the beautiful summer rose
I am the sweet fragrant scent
I am the dreams they came and went
I am the clouds up above
I am the thing that you call love
I am the one that you feel near.
Never forget me.
I am always here.

The Curse
Jon Wright

Born of blooded tears
Mind broken by invisible spears
Shaped by murderous intent
As my dreams become undreamt

Taken in a fit of rage
Soul pulled from its cage
Anger fills the room like blood
As soul flowed like a flood

The candle flickers no more
No more the waves wash the shore
The song in its final verse
Too late, for is born the curse.

Remembrance
Sarah Joy Holden

For so many there are so few
Still they fight for me and you
On the frontline they are called
Their duty to serve and defend

Wrapped in death and sorrow
Tears fall from the grieving widow
From all the wars of yesterday
And those that continue tomorrow

What is this that we strive for peace
As we gather round the cenotaph
Whilst poppies fall in autumn's breeze
For their ultimate sacrifice was death

What does it cost us to stand in silence
For all those we knew and did not know
At the yearly service of remembrance
In the battle fields where poppies grew

We will remember them....

Café Therapy
Sarah Sansbury

Over coffee, she confided
all her tearstained hopes and dreams:
her whole life so lopsided,
bruised, and broken at the seams.
On and on they talked together
of the puzzle of their days,
wondering how, when, or whether
they would navigate the maze.
No easy answers surfaced then,
perhaps they never would;
but still dear friends will meet again
where the coffee tastes so good.

In the Midst of the Stormy Sea
Stasha Strange

In the midst of the stormy sea,
Where the waves rise high and free
Stands a tower tall and strong
A beacon that's been there all along
It's a lighthouse in the raging tide
A symbol of hope dark and wide
Guiding ships through the choppy seas
to safety and peace with ease
The winds may howl and
the rains may pour
The waves may crash on
the rocky shore
But the lighthouse stands
firm and bright
A guiding star in the
darkest night
Its light cuts through the
fog and mist
A ray of hope that can't be missed
Calling out to those in need
A promise of safety
a helping lead
For those who sail the
stormy seas
The light is a gift of ease
A guide that never fades away
A constant in the ebb and sway
So when you're lost in
life's tumultuous waves,
Remember the lighthouse
that always saves
A symbol of hope in times
of despair
A guiding light that's
always there

An Unrequited Love
Kelli Walker

An unrequited love
Is not a quiet thing

It's the constant chippering
Background chatter
Drowning the sound of what once mattered

It's a mumbled grumble
Beneath the breath
Wallowing whispers to the deaf

It's a three a.m. wail
Insomniac alarm
Alerting the heart of imminent harm

An unrequited love
Is the loudest thing
No one ever hears

Afterglow
Sheila Grenon

Before the pulsing hearts begin
Affections are never cast in sin
True efforts brought forward
Heart beating with looks admired

During our sensual escapades
Rarest of moments truly sincere
Love like ours don't compare
To the destinies we have shared

After our passionate fervor
In the small town of Aachen
You being quite debonair,
Had my heart in palpations.

Moon in My Hand
Donna Smith

I clasp the moon in my hands,
It illuminates all that hides in the shadow.
Casting light upon all within my vision,
A wondrous gift it does bestow.

I hold the shine of the sun in my eyes,
It sprinkles iridescent stardust abound.
It lights my footsteps wherever I tread,
Son et Lumiere forms on the ground.

I reach for the shimmering stars,
Through the inky black they show me their light.
Their lustre gleams guiding me onwards,
Providing a small glint, chink into the night.

I grasp for the cumulus clouds,
As they form white cotton balls in the sky.
They cushion and cosset as I journey forward,
Reforming and changing as I pass on by.

I embrace the world underneath my feet,
It leads me down new paths and road.
Guides me in the right direction,
Dust off my shackles, release my heavy load.

Serengeti
Amanda Wilson

Acacia trees under orange skies,
palette at dawn, Serengeti on fire.
The wild savannah with African eyes,
awakening nature stirs as it cries.
Amber breeze lilting a warm zephyr.

Endless plains, the abundant wild landscape.
Tanzania's treasure, sunrise escape.

The rhythm of life, the call of the wild.
Wildebeest throng in ochre dust sand.
Giraffes and Zebras, Hyenas reviled,
tree of life shades on the Lion's pride land.
Eland and Topi on 'Seren' grassland.
Leopards elusive, camouflaged, concealed.
Grumeti river, crocs lay unrevealed.

Giraffes, they pace, can Impala outrun?
Lion voracious, his pride to provide.
On this occasion the Lion is outdone,
Impala guarded, adept, take in stride.
Predator mocked, hunt lost, this time denied.
Cheetahs, Hippos, Rhinoceros, Gazelles,
wildlife reserve, the National Park they dwell.

Green grasses grow, migration, wet season.
Mara traversing, natural world wonder.
Migration to Kenya's Mara region,
Wildebeest thunder, thousands in number.
Herds diminish, Crocs now encumber.
Awaiting migration, ambushing prey,
endangered exposure, making headway.

Masai Mara date trees and red oat grass,
sparsely scattered trees, brushing setting skies.
Blood red sunsets, wildlife sleeping en masse,
predators and prey shutting eyes...
...but soon nature awakes, it stirs and cries.
Another sunrise and seasons will turn,
Serengeti migration to return.

Space Stairs
Neil Mason

Planets wearing carpet slippers
Carrying candles into a purple wilderness
Onwards and upwards on the space stairs
Glitter star footprints left behind on cobweb steps
I fold my astronaut suit and let it sleep on a wooden chair
Slipping in a galaxy of dreams
Sailing a sailboat on a lake of tranquillity
Pass the parcel at the black holes birthday party
Cardboard rockets go further than ever before
A serenade of stardust has many voices
Say good night to yesterday's failures
One more trip up the space stairs
Tomorrow's harbour is yet to be discovered

Complicated
Andy Reay

Outside, we see myriad signals, reactions
The intricate patterns of body language
Flashes of a smile, tongue, red lips
A gesture, a glance

And spoken word, making promises, threats
Choose your words carefully
A sound, an inflection,
the difference between night and day

Inside, voices, thoughts, images
A never ending stream of information
Thoughts provoking nerve impulses, neurons firing
You become anxious, or upset, or aroused

You say some people are complicated
I think we all are

Falling Stars
Stasha Strange

So far down the road
of recovery
Processing triggers
through therapy
found the light
self-loved myself
out of sight
Flipped that implanted
negative chip to
a positive delight
I had only taken flight
where falling stars could
take me out
even in sunlight
Rapid fire triggers
lit up the night
Where processing meets
my inner critic
to discuss my just staying
in and giving up
I've ghosted blood for
making me feel like this...
and even less
Yet here I sit
with silent tears
falling from my eyes.
I thought my journey
went from apathy
to bliss
but here you are
smiling my world apart
back into fear

Dreamt
Fouzia Sheikh

Painted a masterpiece
In my dreams:
A sand Castle
Cactus streams.
A flower composed,
Wilted with time
With muted colours
Tea with lime.
Fields of desert
Winding paths of
Wood and brick flooring.
A cool wind blows
Through the heat
Over sweaty brows
And sandaled feet.
A moment trapped
That's never been.
A life of others
Never seen.
Put away my brushes,
Stood back to admire
The deep ocean sky,
The burnt orange fire.
It lay on the table,
Alive on the canvas
When waking did cause
My hard work to vanish.
In memory only
And never shown
Forever discarded
Once beautifully known.
My studio of mind
So often produces
A wonderful concept
With no practical uses.
I'd like to live there

And run those streets,
But I'll never go there,
Never see that place.
Never plant in soil
That's been erased.
That marvellous day
Conceived at night
Keeps the dreaming
Forever alight.

Abridgment
Tom Cleary

I flit, dart.
Some people call me a flirt
fluttering towards the amber glow
pulsing warmth
ambling towards my soft proboscis
diagnosing hurt.
Possibility resounds
bounds gingerly in its eagerness to redound
yet
pregnant regret
fear long ago set in amber of claustrophobic time
chimes within.
Will your lift over mortal cliff
carry me too high
so that, glancing down
even involuntarily
my wariness reverts to panic
frantic fears of dark depths perceived
conceived in abandonment or absorption?

Your truss allows for mistrust of intent.

Laundry and Rain
Jack H. DeKnight Jr

Laundry and rain
Fresh laundry
New rain
the smells in my brain remain
I love them both
Not how I love you
but both are
pleasant and unseen
The air is clear
the birds are singing
and the grass is so, so green
I can close my eyes and imagine
I can open my heart to the sky
The smell of fresh laundry and rain
Makes me think of you
don't know why

Shine On
Terry Bridges

As this cool evening is temperate
I shed layers of my past with warm tears
Like a snake shedding its skin
Yet the mighty oak grows a new ring every year
Old age becomes me but it's hard letting go
My core being is reduced to diamond ore
And fires up like a glow-worm manufacturing light
Each precious mined nugget of Nature's truth
I weigh in my palm like a talisman
As I journey beyond the darkness's remit

The Amorist
Brandon Adam Haven

Writing alongside sweet roses wedded
Sits a jolly amorist penning his heart
Capaciously dreaming, deeply embedded
Bleeding his soul into the form of art

Deep into the Elysian of blissful thymes
No longer conquered by sorrowful woe
Dulcet are the lines, as the pen still writes
Completely enlivened from his soul

The quintessence of nature imbued
He looks aloft at divinity construed
Overflowing deep into the Everglades
Bright colors, melodic sounds illuminate

By all this, he's completely captivated
His heart vivaciously soft and warm
The feelings of anew, he's anxiously awaited
Spilled in the poetry he intimately forms

Phantom
David Grantz

Shutters clicked, zooms zoomed on either side
of his thin frame, fragile in its frayed sweater
and flapping scarf. He'd gone within his niche,
oblivious to gawking tourists on the deck.
While heads swivelled, his stood still, with eyes
fixed, as if upon some vanishing point before him.
He became context for the crowd, absorbed
within himself, within assembled humanity,
but ignored by those who jostled past, competing
for the perfect spot to take their perfect shot.
I stopped to take mine—of him, my stolen profile of
a secret man—but he sensed intrusion.
Then, like a slender knife, he slipped
into the obscuring crowd.

The Ogre Tree
D. R. Parsons

A mighty great tree, born of a seed,
Witness and abettor to many foul deed.
From this good earth ye did erupt,
Gnarled and knotted and corrupt.
Outstretched arms cast a shadow, dark,
An old face of malice risen on thy bark.
Never has there been any fouler than thee,
Ugly by nature and ugly to see — the Ogre tree.

A great and brutal breach, born of greed,
A different culture, a different breed.
Eight sixty-five, a Northman hoard,
Put to death many with axe and sword.
Vicious minds beget violent times,
Oh cruel Ogre tree to oversee these crimes.
Sent to thy boughs by a Dane decree,
Ugly by nature and ugly to see — the Ogre tree.

A great misdeed, born to mislead,
A few of many, brought here to plead.
A witchfinder general, his dubious law,
A mark she bore proved her witch and whore.
A wife, a husband, a daughter on trial,
As the three of them swung, the tree it did smile.
Dead in thy boughs, fifteen ninety-three,
Ugly by nature and ugly to see — the Ogre tree.

A great and terrible shame, born of need,
The theft of a sheep and a family to feed.
In eighteen hundred, a price deemed fair,
But not by the starving hanging there.
Oh cruel Ogre tree, ye care not why,
A person swings from thy boughs to die.
Thou carest not, a decent man was he,
Ugly by nature and ugly to see — the Ogre tree.

A great and mighty tree, born of a seed,

Witness and abettor to many foul deed.
Standing proud, the biggest of yew,
And as did ye, thy legend it grew.
Futures pass and thou linger on,
Many oak and ash are now long gone.
A shadow, dark, forever cast by ye,
Ugly by nature and ugly to see—the Ogre tree.

Laying Among the Oak
Brandon Adam Haven

Laying among the oak
The leaf tapestry unfettered
A stream of tears beneath
Nature's colorful palette

The streams speak tales
Divine and heavenly glistened
In a language unknown
If you only can listen

Joy within thy heart
Falling into your gaze
Reforming evermore
To brightly change my ways

Symphonies of the soul
Pure and brightly attuned
I'll never go back
To a crumbling world confused

Community Table
Steven Elliott Borodkin

Well of sorrows possess poison
Reflections, dirt, the earth spins
Dead flower, the tired profit, dreams long forgotten
My skin packaged in another, finish line, what to do
We crave insistence of each second that dies
The next second is born with its own story
Tattered books, time reveals life,
life displaces parchment souls
Sun's light the color of eggs.
Coffee as black as my mood.
Toast, wrinkles, jelly, twilight
Age swells, in its own infection
A table of widows, time doesn't wait,
What you've always been shines like a beacon.
A lighthouse guarding us from the dangerous shores.
River of Styx, the weight of water, things washed away.
Dead flower, tired profit, dreams long forgotten,
Breakfast at the community table.

Behind the Willow Tree
Sherry Healy

Like days swarming past, honey dripped from trees fast,
the bees often trapped, ran to escape the cold.

Under great weeping willows I sat generously playing
as if there was no old, no tomorrow to be told.

I played often wearing soft pink dresses or dirty jean overalls, a
cachet for a girl with locks of curly gold, I sat, the ground cold.

Impending loss of youth or will bold to be lost under the weeping
trees, events not wanted or often told by the little girl meeting the
ground cold.

Invasions later to be disgraced as are friars eventually to be cold, their deeds placed beneath the grieving Willows will be told.

Now an extreme requisite for the life of me, a bigger girl, though my youth abused by ugly greeds. New traditions with precious pearls live now, not to be ignored or forced cold.

I am ecstatic, the past is past, I am safe in my sandbox of happiness, my newly pruned Willow tree weeps no more: I have comfort with laughing friends and family. No need to be anything but pleased like honey bees of old, hived at the riverside of bold.

True all bad things eventually end like I was told. Abuse of innocence, too often a sad fact. Certain friars behind trees have died long ago. Though I still have memories, walking to the friar's home of *his* happiness, a tradition of farce, his story now to be told.

Happiness does exist. Life is dear to hold in spite of certain friars lost and old.

For those who don't understand are fortunate. They have no memories like mine, never met friar's hands or spying eyes. Not me, and those who know consequence, not too young or old.

Here I am, shouting the danger toward pink in dresses and overhauls. All children need the right to speak loud of obscenities to be told.

My personal preservations not ignored: life has become beautiful as I find exquisite human compassions of the world. Such love to be found in this life, including my love for the weeping tree who felt for me. I have escaped the ground cold, to thrive as does the golden-green willows of old.

The freshly planted Willow in my backyard is my favorite. I can't help but to love him, as he, like me grows bold. The bees fly freely.

Weeping Orpheus
Madhu Gangopadhyay

Darkness swept
His wife was dead.
Orpheus of Thrace begged and wept;
To the pale moon
As the frayed curtain of night wrapped him;
Biting emptiness engulfed
Music robbed, his heart sobbed:
Calliope couldn't invoke a verse
For her grieving son;
Eurydice was gone
The viper stung,
When in love's swing they swung
Slithering pain
Caustic melancholy,
The venom of separation spread.
What begot such fate?

Aristaeus's fatal chase!
The madly in love couple ran,
The wife fell on the poisonous snake
To the organza moon
Orpheus beseeched for help!
On that ruinous night,
For his lovely wife
He bitterly cried
The moon shed
Tears of grey light
Charcoal vapours of despair
Envy is love's blight

Mess
D. R. Parsons

We've asked you a thousand times before,
Socks and tops and pants on the floor.
Please just for once show that you care,
And shift that dirty underwear.
You turn this house upside down,
Your slippers and your dressing gown.
In every corner there's a shoe,
Is hanging a coat so hard to do?
Can't you see this causes stress?
Please won't you think about your mess!

We've screamed at you many times before,
That goo or glue upon the door.
Those dirty handprints on the wall,
From the attic, downstairs, and through the hall.
Is it so hard to keep things clean?
There's a trail of shite everywhere you've been.
Splatters and spills, not cleaned up,
Dad's trousers smeared with old ketchup.
A greasy stain on mummy's dress,
Please, please...think about this mess.

We've moaned and begged many times before,
A banana skin, rotten apple core.
It never ends and it never stops,
Bottles of pop left without a top.
Pizza, bread and sausage rolls,
Un-scraped plates and dirty bowls.
Our home is filling up with litter,
And stuff like this can make us bitter.
Your attitudes, we must address,
Please...for the love of God, think about your mess.

We've cried and stressed many times before,
Cars and boats, dinosaurs galore.
Playthings spread from wall to wall,
A punching bag and a basketball.

One day soon someone will trip,
Break their hip on a plastic ship.
We cannot see the rug for your toys,
The chaos created by three boys.
Having said all this, I must confess,
Please don't grow up, I might miss this mess.

Green Serene
Graeme Stokes

It's been a while, or so it seems,
my loyal bucolic friend
Since I've cleansed my soul,
in your variegated splendour,
my antidote to heal and mend
I wonder under bashful submission,
humbled in your guard of honour flattery
To grant us this precious time together,
the trust in me to preserve your chastity
As I crunch through your heartfelt offerings,
your verdant generosity
Your irresistible charm, strokes my aching palm,
cuts through my tenebrosity
The cool breeze commands, your ligneous arms,
the trail blows forth a kiss
Your stoic trunks, my champion,
thickets birl in the wilderness
The rays of sun strike your diverse tones,
a multicoloured work of art
The creatures that dwell at your majesty's behest,
revel in their starring part
We walk as one, thoughts pure as snow,
a synchronicity that time forgot
I give thanks, my queen, my green serene,
the lifeblood to my heart!

Sunshine Girl
Kelli Walker

When everything's gone wrong
And writing another lovesick song
Is so much more than you can manage

When angst is your mission
But the crowd's too drunk or bored to listen
I'll be the space where you can place your damage

I will be your sunshine girl
The light down the well
Of your secretive world

I will be your sunshine girl
The thaw on that cold
Indulgence of yours

Yeah, I will be your sunshine girl
The one that sets each night to dream
That you might dream of her

When all the heartache that felt so tragic
Begins to lose its anguished magic
And the message becomes just a mess

When everyone has had enough
You've splintered through your final crutch
And you can't even believe your own press

I will be your sunshine girl
I'll rise up to dry
The rain of your fears

I will be you sunshine girl
Restore your strength
So you can battle your wars

Yeah, I will be your sunshine girl

The one that sets each night to dream
That you might dream of her

Until you've finally absorbed so much of yourself
You're gasping and choking on everything else
And nothing seems deep or sounds profound
In that last wet breath before you drown

I would have been your sunshine girl
I would have brightened your whole damned world
I would have set each night to dream
That you might dream of me

Yeah, I would have been your sunshine girl
I would have set each night to dream
That you might dream of me

Don't Judge
Julie Sheldon

Don't judge a book by its cover
You never know what lies within
Don't judge a child by its mother
We cannot choose how we begin

Don't judge a cake by its icing
It may well be mouldy inside
Don't judge a gift by the wrapping
You never know what it might hide

Don't judge a man by his brother
A gene pool won't make them the same
Don't judge a lord by his title
Don't be overawed by his name

Don't rush to form your opinions
Look deeper beneath the veneer
Endeavour to see the whole picture
Things aren't always as they appear

Vessels
T. M. Warren

Skin fade,
blank eyes,
tattooed teardrops
& gold teeth.
The well-worn mask adorned
by lonesome vessels as they try
and navigate
their way past the 24th hour.
Broken compasses with misdirected energy
veer of track disappearing
into the self-exiled darkness
of their own perceptions.
With reconsideration
the Warrior configuration,
Illuminated by tomorrow's skyline
with all the furnishings of
a modern day Metropolis
in the background.
Preparations are made so to eat...
or to be consumed judging
by the show of hands in the room
& the general consensus.
Regulate your breathing
this is not the audition.
((To horde))
Which fantasy is currently at your residence
taking up space this time?
Creating the cracks as you see
before you whilst reclining back
to admire the work at play.
Watching as they widen and gape
as all light is lost, extinguished.
Allowing forth the dense dark fog
of nihilism to engulf the host.

Bereft of Emotions
Neil Forsyth

Ever imagined what it would be like?
To have no emotions to be unfeeling.
To be devoid, to be diverse of life,
Lost in an absence, without healing.
If anger wasn't angry,
Nor sadness ever sad,
Would happiness make you happy?
No surprise could you have had.
Not disgusted, even shameful,
With lack of satisfaction,
No fear, no awe or envy,
Lacking love or pure reaction.
Being ignorant to pride,
Oh so lost without affection.
Averse to disappointment,
A loneliness distraction
Unable to be worried,
Anxious or annoyed,
Hate-less without jealousy,
Of emptiness, a void.
No boredom or amusement,
Of that being no occasion,
Depleted of embarrassment,
No thoughts of admiration.
Bereft of one's emotions,
No I couldn't care for that,
Life is like an eclectic mix,
That mixes good with bad.

Poetic Waves
Nan DeNoyer

Poetic flow
as the waves
splashing upon the shore
dancing in a rhythm all its own in style.

Its tone
the mood feelings
expressed emotions
as the quill speaks on a gilded white page.

Both are
quite exciting
spoken words of the quill
the sounds of the sea
the written display

Angel
Jinny Morris

Cotton sheets cool on skin
Gently swathed in the cocoon I'm in
Angelic voices whisper softly on the air
Drowsy eyes fixed on lips of a seraphim fair

Cool silken hair sticking to my skin
Wrapping my face until I am captured within
My eyes only free to see the sublime vision
As my mind races in supposition

As lips cover mine as I sink sublime
I never dreamt a kiss like that could be mine
I wake alone way too soon
Wrapped in my lonely cotton cocoon

Mind Medicine
Cate Buchner

When you must leave your loneliness,
take with you, your silence, and your mind's medicine

But remember that it's not far away
One blink and could be back there
The silence can become part of who you are

Scattered around the notes of a book thrown afar
Fall with a thud back to earth
catch the moment for what it's worth
Turn around a thousand times
Look back if you dare
and jump forward towards paradise

A World Without Yellow
Joan Audette

I can't imagine a world without yellow
Can you?

No sunny side egg yolks to greet you in the morn
No butter melting down pancakes
fragrant and warm

No smiley face stickers
on letters you receive
No citrusy lemons
No golden autumn leaves

A life without yellow,
well it just wouldn't do

I can't imagine a world without yellow
Can you?

Catalytic
Markee Reimers

"What do you want to be when you grow up?"
That was a difficult question for me to answer
I wanted to be the cause of change
But not like a doctor, policeman, or a teacher
What I wanted to be was much more profound
But something I bound a buried six feet underground
Because what they forgot to teach me
Was that what I wanted to be didn't have to be
Something monetary
It didn't have to be a career
Or something so sheer
Something that is a mere representation of who I could be
I want to completely alter people with my presence
I want to be a catalyst starting a new sentence
In the lives of others upon my entrance
I want to trigger something inside of people
Something so lethal to their identity
That they begin to question their destiny,
Start to investigate their own tendencies,
And begin to realize that they are their own worst enemy
I want to do this carefully in a way that is unspoken
Where people can just look at me and see the unbroken
I want to cause a commotion
And set in motion what is frozen
Be a coachman to the un-woken
I want the agitation to be caused by my being
That my existence alone can show them meaning
That my attendance brings with it a type of gleaming
That haunts them in the evening and within their dreaming

I want to be the clearest portrayal of hope
I want to paint a picture of a slippery slope
One that can be escaped only by rope
A climb so operose
That in the process I became madder
Until I learned that I mattered
And a sliver of worthiness became a ladder

I want the rope to have written stories on my hands
Scars left behind but is not my brand
To show everyone what can be done
If you refuse to succumb to the gravity of life

Shadows
D. A. Simpson

Shadows of eventide
stretch their limbs
wearied now and in need of slumber
as the hour of evenfall
draws ever nearer

They drift across the sands
edging a lake of crystal waters
exalting in the seclusion of a remote realm

And carpet the deserted beach
gilded by the rays of the setting sun

While thin ribbons of cloud
tinged with the gold of sunset
glide through the impassive firmament

As the tranquil scene
exults in the cool of a serene dusk
roaming the lakeside
Where the poplar trees grow
amid the mysteries of a twilight mist
Written in the language of enigma
as old as time itself

Know This Deer Hart
Jinny Morris

Since you left your blood red smear
across my husk dry heart.
Since the world of safe blindness
cracked and spilled its offal and guts.
All that's female within my soul spluttered,
stopped and won't restart.
The questions that formed
on my deceitful tongue
no longer form ifs or buts.

Since the lines were crossed
by the serpent from Azazel's hand.
Whence it slithered leaving shards
of broken glass under my cloven feet.
My corrupted mouth that once spilled
self-deceit upon demand.
Now spews its truthful admissions
of an unavoidable defeat.

If one day the old bones
of our coitus are dug up.
If my taintedness is washed clean
by your admission of shame.
I will present you a toast
with my poisoned lover's cup.
To send your miscreant soul
into un-sacred darkness once again.

I am not Barren
Shafkat Aziz Hajam

I am not barren.
My fecundity has not dwindled yet.
Enough as before to bring forth
blossoms of all sorts and I do.
Alas ! Frequent invasions of atrocious autumn
Debilitates their potency to bloom in full
To show my greatness in their daintiness and redolence
That would once captivate waves from overseas
To warble in praise of my nature.
O Heaven! Free me from this brutish autumn,
Can't endure it any more.
To glitter with my flair
Let clement spring reign over me.

The Day I Died
Darren B. Rankins

Don't look at me as if I were dead,
just think of me resting in bed.

Now cover me with eternal life
and place my favorite flowers upon my head,
and if the night shall pass
and you miss holding my heart in your hand,
just make a wish upon the nearest star
and there I'll stand.

Now take all my worldly possessions
and give them to the needy
because my riches now lie with God.

Now sing me a love song
as I walk down this lonely road,
and please don't worry because
my Lord waits with opened arms.

Truthfully Yours
Archie Papa

Truth was real, we imagined lies
emotional wool pulled over our eyes
fear was summoned deep from within
and so the illusion of time would begin
Sorting the precious from all we've lost
quicken the pace to bear the cost
racing to nowhere at breakneck speed
blur the line between want and need
The battle for truth was underway
the heart finds words the mind won't say
greed is searching through everything
the rumble and chatter let chaos ring
A distant truth, a glimmer of light
tenacious hope and will to fight
the honest are those who realize
truth is real, we imagine lies

Reflections
Jackie Shaffer

Silence in the moment
Me loving the peace
Old chapters, accruement
Shadows never cease
Sitting and reflecting
Aimlessly, no directing
Minds memories of the past
Things unsaid
Too much said
Heartache and joy
Like two sides of a coin
No changes can be made
Aging, things tend to fade
Silence of those memories
New memories invade

Whispers
Kieran R. Eldritch

Whispers of the wind through a barren moor,
The creaking of an empty chair on a forgotten floor.
Footprints fade in a desert vast,
Echoes of laughter, shadows of the past.

Moonlight paints a silvered street,
But no warmth to greet, no souls to meet.
A solitary candle in a window pane,
Flickers in the cold, extinguished by rain.

Leaves fall with no one to watch their descent,
A silent lament, in solitude spent.
An untouched piano, its keys gather dust,
Its melodies silent, its strings full of rust.

In the vastness of night, where dreams are undone,
There's an absence of light, no place for the sun.
The world turns, but some corners remain,
Where silence is loud and solitude's pain.

Untamed Emotions
Rafik Romdhani

Life waters me and on paper
grows my thoughts,
The scythes of sorrow
to my neck, like the claws of birds.
Fire never ceases breathing
and climbing my feral eyes
propelled with sailors and their oars.
Life opens up more rusty doors
each time untamed emotions
put a dent in my edgy heart.
Life waters me with more
than the brokenness in clouds
because it already knows
that for every pain I tailor
a pretty costume from words.

Before Morning Twilight
Geoff Edwards

When the moon and the stars
come to play with the sun,
like czars the wistful trees
adjudicate the whereon.

Serenely sitting on a silent hillside,
huddled under a cosy comforter,
bundled bodies bracing against
the cold, immobilizing hush,
the slitting stillness of a scoreless symphony
and the tacit splitting

starkness of the dark against the light.
The demons of the night melt away
grasping claws on the fading night
the probates of dark now to pay
the light vanquishing the blight

Perforated veil tears on the continuum
between the coal mine black brooding silhouetted trees,
standing, waiting, wanting, for a candescent spark
and the celestial splendour of tiny teardrops of
twinkling stars, *now* there — pale-yellow ribbons forcing,
prying, splitting the dark asunder!

The demons of the night melt away
grasping claws on the fading night
the probates of dark now to pay
the light vanquishing the blight

Slowly sauntering, the snails of Apollo
continuing climbing constantly upward unyielding to the
colossal dark, snails *no now* winged horses canter,
whip cracks, bridle loosens, hoof beat faster
hooves blazing, dark shatters, — into cathedrals of bird chorus

smashing the silence, —on on the
blazing chariot, up onward up, gallop galloping,
powerfully pulling, propelling, the dripping sweat of
muscles in motion setting the sky ablaze,
travel travelling scattered scattering the dark denied.

Morning glories open wide
sunflowers heads they turn
the brooding trees abide
now, no longer yearn.

London
Tony Dukeva

London, London—a city of grace
A city of fast pace, a magical space
A city of royalty, a city of mystery
Crowned in beauty, a city of history

Charming pubs and tea shops invite
To savour a pint or a cosy respite
To eagerly indulge in the dazzling sight
To see all the colours that light up the night

The symbolic Big Ben keeps an eye on time
And counts double-deckers on the gridded lines
The London eye mixes the sky and the land
And makes you forget all that you planned

London, London—a city of grace
Whispers of art in every trace
Passions and dreams in every face
Restyling of spirit in this urban space

Marble Smasher
Genevieve Ray

Read the palmar flexion
The creases in human cloth
The trenches that are pine coloured
Born to mould
Born to fashion
Unaccustomed to chisels
Made to hold pencils

Marble smasher
Antiquity will quiver
The utensils motion
To decimate antique mentalities

Read the palmar flexion
Paste-white palms
Shaped human skin
Out of bold, proud cubes
Building out nightmare screams
Almost audible entreaties
Caught in forever paused throats

Marble smasher
Antiquity will quiver
The utensils motion
To decimate antique mentalities

Read the palmar flexion
Flooded with blue or black ink
Able to give Prospina argument
Conscious of Ophelia's fury
Returning Cleopatra's sadness
Lead forth the unnamed girl
And return her to thought-filled woman

Marble smasher
Antiquity will quiver
The utensils motion
To decimate antique mentalities

Marble smasher
Antiquity will quiver
Calliope's borrowed pen
Giving new souls empowerment

Dark Times
Minka Leeser

Will there be poetry
In the dark times?
Yes, there will be poetry
Because of the dark times.
Will there be dreams
In the dark times?
Yes, there will be dreams
Because of the dark times.
Will there be songs
In the dark times?
Yes, there will be songs
Because of the dark times.
Will there be praying
In the dark times?
Yes, there will be praying
Because of the dark times.
Will there be stories
In the dark times?
Yes, there will be stories
Because of the dark times.
Will there be an end
In the dark times?
Yes, there will be an end
Because of the dark times.

Mending
Rhiannon Owens

The sea squalls, gulls shriek...
Hard in these parts
Calloused fingers pull ropes taut,
Wood sawn and planed; chiselled all day

A funny place to mend a broken heart
To start anew, a funny place these parts,
Hard to mend a broken heart...

Family histories, community
The Shipping News...
Car wrecks, boat wrecks, lunatics
Paltry offerings to make the locals tick

Lobster pots and clubbing seals,
Another son lost to the waves
Sun reflecting off turquoise and teal

Icebergs and snow drifts
Boats sucked astray,
Baked bread, wild parties and Christmas pageantry
In this Newfoundland way

So hard to learn that love is not pain
So hard to survive in hard conditions
To survive in these parts...

Welcomed, accepted
Finding your niche,
A tall, quiet woman
Calm waters flood your heart...

Under a streaked, reflective sky
Echoes a humped ancient sigh,
This island's whale song;
A place to finally belong

Suddenly, you glance at her
Her weathered skin
Her wry smile,
An accordion, children dancing
Everything is in reach...

Leave the flotsam and jetsam
Just one more wreckage...
Forgotten driftwood of your past
Decaying on the beach

poetry never sleeps
Matthew Elmore

I laid my head on a weary poem for a bed
frozen with hot emotions of notions withdrawn
earth mocked blue sky, water cursed black ice
as dusk undressed red to mate sedate dawn
fire flirted with flame of ambiguous shame
textured lectures frayed fabrics of my mind
of value in verses; imagery penned in hearses
under blankets rewinding unproven paradigms
pillow of woe feed frivolous glow to an old crow
bereft of wind under dark un-feathered wing
let a canopy be set to divert bleary tears wept
by clouds this melancholy muse longs to sing
loosen these lines bound binary and benign
isolating my violated isolation succinct
brighten my way with similar opposites play
upon sleep I keep to creep upon that brink

How do You say Goodbye?
Joan Audette

How do you say goodbye
to a house, a home, a haven?

'Twas a quaint cosy place
embracing comfort

a sanctuary where you were free
to be just you

Where love was discovered,
love shared, love lost

tears shed, laughter loosed;
deaths mourned, births rejoiced

But now the season of change
is upon us

No longer will our voices
ring from the walls

nor our feet
make their way up the steps

This part of life has passed;
will remain a honeyed memory

But how, oh how, do you say goodbye
to a house, a home, a haven?

Losing You
Lorna McLaren

I know you don't remember me,
but I love you all the same,
though every now and then you will
quietly speak my name.
You gaze through those unseeing eyes,
I can't imagine what you see
even though your gaze has fallen
directly on to me.
Almost childlike in your way,
frightened and unsure,
wish I could get inside your head
to see what you endure.
I'd love to hold you close to me,
the way you held me in your arms,
but every time I get close to you
in your eyes I see alarm.
The you I knew is no longer there
even though you look the same,
I cry inside on losing you
but by your side I will remain.

Sadako – Hiroshima 1955
Sarah Sansbury

Her automatic hands pleat rainbow squares
evening breeze whispers through Sakura
another tiny crane takes flight
to join its many brothers
until a thousand friends
have wings for their pain
as morning breaks
she's folded
into
peace

I Stand/I Cry/I Fly
Shirley Rose

When I have fallen, I can no longer stand
You gently take me by the hand
You lead me out of muck and mire
Through wind and smoke and raging fire
Through briar and bramble you cut a swathe
Which leads to the sea so I can bathe
Wash off my shame and mess and stain
Be dead to sin, be free again
And now I fly on eagle's wing
My heart is light, Your song I sing
Higher and higher my soul takes flight
Not stuck in stinking sinking mud,
I'm light as a feather.
I soar on thermals of rising air
And soon, very soon, I will be
There, where You reside in
Power, love and peace
From this humbled body, grant me release!

Happiness Within
Joel Aparecio Bernasor

Delighting arise with happiness
Contentment begets sans joyfulness
Not gaining worldly materials
Or occupying inside specials,
Evocation to joviality
Of hearts content sans vivacity
Happiness elated from within
Through expression like a chain,
Happiness lead to eudaimonia
Shared to all in path of gardenia
Harmony, solidarity align
In every heart flourish and reign

Lone Figure
Lorna McLaren

In long brown robes of sackcloth
with rope tied for a belt,
cross hanging low from round his neck,
a heavy weight is how it felt.

Head bowed low he walks the grounds,
arms crossed tucked in his sleeves,
he feels the crunch beneath his sandaled feet
of the fallen Autumn leaves.
So slowly does he amble round,
quite silent in his prayer,
a lonely Friar taking stock,
for no-one else is there.

The friary crumbles round him,
for centuries have gone,
roof now open to the elements
no longer rings with chant-like song.
The voice that once spoke loud and clear
is silenced in his grief,
the price he paid, his penance,
for questioning his belief.

If you're ever at the Friary and see
a lone figure dressed in brown
it will be the spectre of the Friar
destined to forever walk the grounds.

Be respectful of his plight,
don't look away in fear,
he'll bless you as you pass on by
and drop a doleful tear.

Afternoon
Jeff Goodman

Afternoon
Newly paved
Black asphalt
Desert tar
August
Motorcade
Pile Up
Behind a
Slow moving
Truck
Moving Slowly
Opposite
Westward bound
Direction home
My hometown
Landmark in sight
Up ahead

Run
Mike Rose

When I was young
I could run really fast
I'd race the sun all day
At night I'd sleep on the grass

I'd lay under the stars
And just watch them shine
With a smile on my face
And nothing on my mind

These days I wish
I could run that fast
The first place I'd run

Is straight to the past

I'd blow through the years
Just like the wind
Come in for a landing
And do it all over again

I want to feel
How I felt back then
The world was beautiful
Everyone was my friend

I want to run free
I want to run wild
I want to see the world
Through the eyes of a child

Release the Spirit
Sarfraz Ahmed

Never afraid of falling
As long as I can fly first
As long
As I can quench my thirst
Spread my wings
Breathe in
Breathe out
See what life's all about.
Let me shimmer
Let me shine
Let me intertwine
Touch the light fantastic
Watch me surf
Watch me glide
Release the spirit
From deep inside.

The Day the Light Went Out
Kirsty Howarth

I remember that day
The day the light went out
Someone flicked a switch
And no one heard me shout
I remember feeling frightened
As I heard the news you'd gone
Stumbling in the dark
Trying to put the light back on
Frozen and confused
Unaccepting of your end
Putting down the telephone
I had lost a friend
Suffocating in despair
Struggling to breathe
My heart pounding way too fast
Not knowing how to grieve
But yet I'm surviving
Trying to find my way
Trying to find a rainbow
In the sky so grey
They'll never be a pot of gold
And my rainbow's far away
Yet I keep on travelling
As I know I'll make it there some day
I see brightness in the distance
And that's what gives me hope
I have companions on my journey
And that's what helps me cope
I know you are beside me
I believe that this is true
You stayed to bring me comfort
And I often talk to you
I've cried so many tears
And I still scream and shout
My world was left in darkness
The day the light went out

Youth Potion
Sherry Healy

Soil filled with a seed of hope and memory
A garden once existed there
The dirt in my hand might hold a past notion
A youth potion
A clean smell of air
Once a time
Tomatoes and corn grew there
The seasons did time
Nothing in the dirt went unmined
Mud came when the earth rained
I did not mind
The mild of heat took care of that
I sat and watched the tomatoes grow
I loved them so
My hand help that soil
I love it still

Soulmates
Minka Leeser

As I entered the room
I spied you standing there
just a few feet away
Our eyes locked in place on one another.
A feeling of eternal familiarity swept over us
You came to me and took my hands,
our eyes never breaking their stare
finding and embracing one another's souls
The butterflies in our beings burst out of their
cocoons
refusing to be contained
and flew out of every pore,
as our souls spoke to one another through the ether.
We kissed and sealed our fate.
Soulmates

Tranquil Night
Kenneth Wheeler

How still and silent is this perfect night
where nothing loud resounds as it might.
No noises, passing planes or roaring motor bikes
to disturb the precious peace of this tranquil night.

I will sleep until the morning sun invades,
slowly creeping up across my window panes.
The warmth of my bedding and the pillow 'neath my head
add to the pleasure of a tranquil night abed.

Abyss
Sheri Lemay

Darkness creeps in
Swirling around
Seeping in and out
An endless dance
Between joy and despair
Walking that fine line
Between life and death
Emotions churning
Exhaust sets in
A decision to be made
Emerge into the sun
Or fall into the bottomless abyss
How easy it would be
To welcome the darkness
Snuff out the light
Just fade away
No longer a burden
A weight gone from the world

Wild Beasts
Joe Mendoza

My anxiety isn't just
The elephant in the room.
It's also the hippo
In the car
The monkey
In the kitchen
The spider
In the restroom
The lion
In the living room and
The snake
That wraps itself around me
At night as I lie in bed
Struggling to fall asleep.
My anxiety never leaves me.

It's like something
I've grown weary of but
Don't know how
To get it to leave.

I'm afraid of being left alone.
I wasn't always this way but
On the day you left
You didn't just take my heart
You took my mind with you also.

And left me wandering
In this jungle all by myself.

My Name is Rage
Pureheart Wolf

There is an unrest
A hunger that awaits with each breath,
There is a darkness
No light can enter here, the blackness eludes.
Deep, in the depths a barren womb.
The calm covers the anguish,
The eyes are lost, in a hypnotic trance
The rage bubbles as if boiling on hot coals,
Every day she awakes
Painted smiles, eluding but alluring guise.
The pain that she carries
A heavy burden that no one knows.
A cross to carry, for the sins that she holds.
You may see her look your way
An ordinary woman, with not a great deal to say
She walks between the shadows
and hides from your gaze
Count yourself lucky,
that she holds onto that rage.

Remembrance
R. David Fletcher

I cried sweet tears for all those years,
When I looked into her eyes,
And lost my dreams in infinity scenes,
When I found out she had died.

Never Earth
Adookorn Adookorn

Never earth in awesome costume flaunt;
With painterly art of embroidery lace
Sea and sky gussy up chromatic earth
Awaiting callous sun his resurgence
As moon to the womb of dawn seek rebirth
My love moon on lap of caressing night
In patience let me wait her nascence
Though cauterise sun swank radiance bright;
My still soul seek not a scourging fiancé
On this lone beach my sober moon shall bight;
Let me wait, wait for my lulu embrace
And smear her fragrance of roses at twilight
Rinse off foul sweat and taunting sun replace
Wait on this lone beach for my lulu embrace
And smear her fragrance of roses at twilight!

Low Sky
Anna Obara

Too many words
noise in my head
I guard dreams
from getting out of control
inhale exhale
apnoea tear
love in veins
flowing upstream
despite the weakening arteries

Today
when my heart beats are credited
the sky is so low...

A Chorus of Sunflowers
Janet Stoyel

Ragged, impasto, fire-kissed cumulus clouds
dot a summer sunset sky
Drifting down low confetti-like,
no intention to fall or cry
A soft earthbound heavenly breeze
descending from way-up-there-on-high,
Smears a thick slurry pastiche
of striated cirrus, colourful stains, rich and royal,
Textural three-dimensional —
catching, reflecting incandescent light,
Kaleidoscopic magnificence of glorious tumbling night.
Rich capitula florets circle wide —
Fibonacci perfection in replication,
Floral faces framed in petalled collars
of fluttering golden hue
Helianthus annuus to botanists —
flowers of international nobility,
Descended from the perennial daisy ….
sunflowers to me and you.
In a field under the glowering summer —
dusk of half-light,
In syncopated rhythm ….
cerulean petiolate leaves ripple,
Swaying, in heliotropic gyration,
they slowly turn the opposing way ….
Tall flowers dancing in the darkness
to pass the night away.
Lifting sleepy heads in anticipation
of the fast-approaching dawn
Faces tilt, confronting the East,
absorbing first light and heaven's warmth.
There is inherent mystery
and beauty to be found
in a field of sunflowers.

School Reunion
Genevieve Ray

Our twenty years are up
A gap of decades
Sparse lives and names
Half of the population
They used to shorten ties
And alter white shirts
Now they double their surnames
The prefects may nod
In slight remembrance
Our graduating class glut
Of prefecture expansion
Those who always interrupted
Are now soldiers and mothers
The quiet ones are entrepreneurs
Awaiting questions
On partnership and parentage
Proxy markers of adulthood
The dotted map borne
Of maturity travelled
Champagne rites
And tissue papered tables

In plain-spoken words
Sawn into wooden desktops
"Do you still fancy Jimmy?"
"Did you marry Michael?"
"Did Shubad become a popstar?"
Passing notes on success
Playground life-list-chase

An elevated chortle
Over a Sainsburys; wine glass
For polite shared memories
Final thought under disco lights
"I do not remember why I came"
"I do not remember her name"
That sweet faced sixteen-year-old

The Girl in the Mirror
Kirsty Howarth

The girl in the mirror
Not who she used to be
A girl who has lost her way
And her beauty she cannot see

Her body now a skeleton
And gone is the girl that we once knew
She's seeking perfection
From photos so untrue

Flawless skin and toned and thin
And nowhere cellulite
Pressured by the media
To look perfect and just right

Skipping meals to lose more weight
And excessive exercise
Obsessive and dangerous
To get the gap between her thighs

The women in the magazines
Admired by many men
They are her inspiration
As she's self-harming yet again

Her health has deteriorated
And her spark lost from within
Exhausted and frustrated
As all she wants to be is thin

Botox injections in her face
To keep the lines away
And keeping up with fashion
And debt for these she has to pay

Creams, lotions and diet pills
And make up from high end brands

Striving for perfection
Just as society demands

Her expectations are unachievable
And she feels disappointed, sad and crushed
She cannot seem to understand
That the models photos are airbrushed

Her inner demons are too strong
As she keeps trying to get thinner
And every day she battles
With her reflection in the mirror

Things
Sarah Sansbury

My pocket rectangle
knows things about me:
which shampoo I use,
how I drink my tea;
the books I've bought,
the fish I've caught,
everything I've said,
last year's holiday address,
what time I go to bed.
You'd almost think it's tracking me
for some malicious purpose …
but then it winks seductively
and smooths over the surface.
Fellow travellers unawares
are also mesmerized,
clicking tiny coloured squares
and hoping for a prize.
I can't shake off a somewhat
indefinable sensation
that rectangles are hatching plots
for worldwide domination.

I am the little I am
Matthew Elmore

expanding horizons on depreciating lands
paying tolls into portals; I am the little I am
supernova exploding, patrolling arid sands
on mountaintops of supplication now I stand
seasoning seasons of creations born too bland
glorifying a greater story; I am the little I am
celebrating songs relating woman to man
a pebble in great oceans; I am the little I am
long before this current big bang ever began
I existed under wild wings; I am the little I am
humbled by grace, overpowering the damned
strengthened by spirit; I am the little I am
commissioned to a mission eternally planned
collecting different colors; I am the little I am
sentinel over space ways of seas forever swam
ambassador to passion; of desire most grand
endearing comparisons of souls in one hand
not mine but of one that is greater than I am…

The Passion of the Rose
Patricia Woosley

Oh! The lovely red, red rose.
Her radiant beauty is beyond compare.
She is as soft and delicate
as an angel's wings,
floating gently in the morning air.
Her deep red petals,
like a lover's passion,
create a desire to be touched,
but her thorns warn,
"Caress me oh, so very gently,
for true love cannot be rushed."

Strange Cacophony
Steve Wheeler

Our lives form strange cacophonies
of motions blurred inside a liquid dream;
the quicklime magic fails as statues freeze
each folding hour, another Wilhelm scream

far out beyond forbidden fractured flare,
the antelope leaps high o'er open graves,
cavorting wildly through the solid air,
avoids the bolted cauldron's mist cascade

the solemn fog obscures a mind impure
defying reason, cold from columned sense,
within that vessel, vivid truths obscure,
whose residue dries up in realms immense

surprised, the soul breaks from its solemn mould,
it writhes and twists, bombastic in ballet,
and as the wildéd forest boughs unfold,
beholds the form in garish green array

oh damn! this scolding skein of reverie
unravels twisted torture born anew,
metallic tendrils stretch their twisted spree
dispelling what the fallen angels knew

Somewhere's Someone
Jeff Goodman

There always
Seems to be
A missing book

A sign that
Everyone ignores
A cry no one hears

A language few
Speak and fewer
Care for

Anger going
Absolutely nowhere
Downtown

Down misty
Roads leading
Towards dream lands

Illusion that
Sparks wars
Delusions lived

By
Astonishment
Barely covers

Absence
Imelda Zapata Garcia

Crowded halls, hold up walls, sheltering
tender tendrils for the sake of survival
darkness creeps into hidden corners
allowing lighter shades for exposure
bright, superficial visage, centers veneer
permits pleasantries upon arrival
reality is shrouded as struggle ensues
while war rages on neath full composure

in distant roaming a heft weighs heavy
presenting fissures in increments
shredding takes place amid revelries
serving as sustenance for vows
a hunger, a wanting, encroaching settles
allowing ravages within consent
treading water in the land of palm trees
breathing in whispers while time allows

Sand is insurmountable, no escaping
the rigours shift the sifting of plans
sunrise lifts sagging pupils upward
offering promise to sunsets encumber
high on the ether, surrounded by love
a fleeting spirit, traversing in trance
wades in pools of pleasure, soaking
embracing leisure in slumber

Street Punctuation
Geoff Edwards

Random rambles down the road
hopping there to here like a toad.
Chaos curiously looks around
eyes down ever looking around.

Half listen in the crowded street,
Random; speaks about a dude named Pete
dissonance waiting at the cash machine wall
Chaos; shaping the order of it all

White tipped cane tapping the street.
Half; turns following the beat,
order brought for sitting guest,
Dissonance; positions plates per request

Mother and child play peek-a-boo,
White; giggling at the view.
Poetry, ballet of the marketplace
order, random, chaos embrace.

Iridescent
Pritha Lahiri

Sometimes crimson
    Sporadically grey
Always smitten
    Heart sways
Often aquamarine
    The sky preens
Iridescence umpteen
    Empyrean domain
Celestial twain
    Magna attain
Heavenly reign.

Love
Kirsty Howarth

Love is like a snowflake
Melting on my face
Love is like a ballerina
Dancing, full of grace
Love is like a raindrop
Falling from the sky
Love is like a promise
To never say goodbye
Love is like the summer sun
And an autumn breeze
Love is like newness in spring
And a winter freeze
Love is like the chorus
Of the birds singing at dawn
Love is like fresh cut grass
After the mowing of my lawn
Love is like the aroma
Of ground coffee beans
Love is like the comfort
From my favourite pair of jeans
Love is like the moisture
Of the fresh morning dew
Love is like completeness
Love is me and you

Phoenix from the Dark
Amanda Marchuk

In the depths of my being, anxiety takes hold,
A haunting reminder of childhood trauma untold.
Memories etched deep, scars unseen,
A burden carried, a constant, relentless machine.

The weight of the past, a heavy load,
Intrusive thoughts, like a relentless ode.
Heart racing, palms sweating, breath shallow,
Anxiety's grip, unyielding, hard to swallow.

Childhood innocence shattered, dreams torn,
The echoes of trauma, forever worn.
Yet amidst the darkness, a glimmer of light,
Resilience and strength, a will to fight.

Through therapy and healing, I find my way,
Unravelling the knots, day by day.
Anxiety may linger, but I refuse to be defined,
I reclaim my power, my peace of mind.

For in the depths of my being, I find solace,
A reminder of the strength within, a promise.
Childhood trauma may have left its mark,
But I rise above, a phoenix from the dark.

Inheritance
T. M. Warren

Archaic identities
& the psychic lives of our ancestors.
Unknowable to outside agencies.
"Have you been communing
with my late Father?"
The sorrowful mysteries
& the tender mercies.

Mission creep

This program has been accelerated!
A Father's message
& the unwanted inheritance
from beyond the grave
delivered to the son via the sanguine.
A Familial curse born
from an alchemical romance
that produced
Greatness &
...deformed red blood cells.
From the past comes the
present that dictates
the future.
I am sanctified
with all your revelations.
The beauty & the uncertainty.
The Perusha
—That single
binding unity behind
everything that exists
in the Universe.

Walk With You
Mike Rose

Take my hand
I'll walk with you
Through the rain
Under skies of blue

Down that path
Around the bend
Start at the beginning
Staying till the end

Take the crooked road
That leads far away
Mark that trail
Follow it back someday

Face the hard times
Look for easier ways
Because life is short
Even in its longest days

The Kingdom
T. M. Warren

To blanket this unknown participant
the misunderstood schizophrenic
with disdain & derision
is a fruitless endeavour
& a foolish move.
Caught between 2 worlds
the torn fabric of the veil
once rigid & held in authority.
Now unrecognisable
worn down,
weary
from age & the responsibility

It once held.
The sentry guard asleep
at its post.
Dreams from the past
merge with the present.
Memories bypass the 2nd brain
the (G.I tract)
& flood the individual
with images of a time
when it was entrusted
to guard over this
firmament
which in turn it was accountable for.
This Kingdom
Where everything was held
In its rightful place
now deconstructed
& fragmented.

Colour perception
is predetermined to the individual
e.g.: green = passivity
add to that
the propensity for pattern recognition.
{Side note}

**Our coercive measures
must remain undetected.**

Following on with
weaponised linguistics
& dark techniques
i.e.: lies, propaganda,
false symbology through images.
Heavy distortion
which invokes
& entices
the Circus to come to town.
So in closing
have sympathy for the
Veil & the fragility that comes with it.

Rowdy Day
Adookorn Adookorn

I do not envy the rowdy day
Fade away with madding crowd,
Their monstrous craving and bay

At rebirth weary sun goes to bed
For whose reign silence sing praises
With processions of fairies and owl

In tranquil whisper has arisen —
Caresses the poet in me to purl
You, stygian painterly sombre lover

I solemnly solicit your presence
O! Night, let me in your bath shower
And smear the redolence of silence

Bottle in the musing of my heart;
Let me into eerie sea deep plunge,
From the archive of the gods beneath

Where lay the knowledge to salvage
Steal the aesthetic art of wisdom
Mortal man his vanity bridle

Let me have my lyceum in your bosom
And solve the equations of life riddle!

R.I.P. No Epitaph Burden
Hahona Pita Batt

Ichor laden mists
satiate solitary confine
My once adroit
emollient grail
refuses to
oxygenate sourstuff
Thy burgundy chalice
excoriates in
spendthrift refrain

Thine carapaced effigy
thirsts for needled relief
A diaphanous desolate
gossamer firmament
arraigns notional gravitas

Tumbleweed mind jaunt
distilled in cactus brine
Phosphorus whispers
fail to ignite
existential cognizance

Top shelf notions splutter
in backfired ameliorate
Roman sandal retrograde
incites toe jammed saunter

Crucifix visions of salvation
plied in last breath desperation
Wineskin dry
& twice as obtuse
Frayed enlightenment
in bankrupt conjugation

Dry retch
in striated aperture
Fractured jaw

in toothless maw
Life drains
from jaundiced corpuscle
Barbiturate permutations
wagered in
crepuscular foreclose

Brave but for feats
of cowardice
Tepid dyke
evacuated fingers
embalm an
enervated mind

Thine mind meld mesmeric
sailing ship sojourn
neath toothpick
skeletal bones

Sutured skin scrawl
cauterizes any notion
of edification
Purgatory disseminates
fornicating nugatory notions

A sanctimonious
Cyclops Pirate
infiltrates my
seminal discourse
Cursed in ocular deficit
wassailing Medusa decrees
in one eyed flaccid gloat

Green mile
boughs sag
in anticipation
of the final onslaught
Walking the plank
in desert
mirage infirmary

The proscenium curtain call...
an amorphous oblation
A spendthrift effigy
hewn prostrate & bereft

No epitaph burden
in Davey Locker's
ichor acute
brain fade
matriculate!

We All Find Our Peace
Patricia Woosley

An old dried-out rose
on his long-forgotten grave,
is now covered with dirt;
No memories are saved.
No one comes to visit
the weed-covered ground.
His deserted tombstone
can hardly be found.
Many years have gone by,
and his face has grown dim.
No longer is there pain.
No one cries over him.
No one ever mentions his name.
He's gone and forgotten
No, nothing remains.
We've all moved on,
and gone on with our lives.
Life is all about living.
That's how we survive.
It's too sad to hold on
to what used to be,
so God makes a new way,
and we all find our peace.

The Wrath of the Devil
Andy Allen

The devil's burning breath blistered
The cold skin on my back.
The ghosts of bad choices
Chased me down dark alleys.
The spectres of unkind deeds
Pursued me through the night.
The shadows of a hundred crimes obliterated daylight,
And I ran from the wrath of the devil
Straight into your open arms.

Your bosom offered harbour;
A new beginning at your hearth.
A last chance for redemption
And to exorcise my past.
I drank in your tranquillity
Grew fat on peace of mind
I lounged around your cushioned goodness
And bathed in warm intent.

But your light burned too brightly
So that all but you were blind.
Your way was the only path
From which no man is to veer.
Your holy dominance, sadistic
In its well-intentioned fervour.
The suffocating kindness
Of unselfishness and prayer
Grated on my troubled soul
'Till I could no longer bear.

And though I'd escaped the devil's wrath
I turned in search of hell.
I found forgiveness in its fires
And guidance in its scorn.
I snuffed out your righteousness
For the darkness from before
For the furious wrath of the devil
Is what I live for.

Essential Oil
David Grantz

He would paint on days like this,
Winds cavalcading through fields,
Jostling the olives in swaying branches,
Blue-green waxen leaves, jerking.
How the gusts swirl the Cypresses,
Whipping these Provencal fields,
Whistling the ramparts, begging escape
From vine-knitted sanitorium walls.
But this is spring, so no yellow grain;
Red buds and almond blossoms flock
Cloître Saint Paul, its twisting cypresses
Hungry for canvas — the exhilaration!
Then — depression, for no woman comes,
And the charted rabble goes faceless
At safe distance. Only the natural for him,
On such days when hair and trees blow wild,
Scattering acid and anguish from
The sanctuary of the inner breath.

The Irish Wind
Jannetta Lamort

You have been picking blackberries in the dusty hedgerows —
fingers stained with their juices, flavoured by your summer rain.
I enjoy your delight in these last warm days —
reflected in a reddened nose and forehead.
You remark that the mornings are cooling —
and plan one more swim.
I see your toes gripping the cool, damp sand —
the ocean curving the beach into the mountain'd skyline.
You will paint the cottage against the winter storms —
protecting your family memories — a magical place.
I envy the Irish wind —
kissing along the nape of your neck.

Seas and Life
Lorna McLaren

Crashing waves against the shoreline
disturbing seaweed in its wake,
a soft wind brushing, passing over,
as if intent, rage to placate.
Ebbing tides that amble slowly,
shifting sand and moving scree,
taking with it all its secrets
carrying them back out to sea.
The ebb and flow of tides are timeless
following phases of the moon,
singing its melancholic aria
of danger lurking in its womb.
It has the power to soothe the mind
and yet take life without a thought,
no conscience has the wayward ocean
but neither does it have a plot.
And as it journeys on relentlessly
I often wonder at its power
as I find it is a contradiction,
it can be sweet and yet be sour.
Life itself can seem no different
with changing moods and unseeing eyes
for there is no true way of knowing
whether the good or bad will rise.
Try always then to be respectful,
stay humble, for after all,
if you think that you're above all others
that could bring on your downfall.
Life and seas they intermingle
as we travel through our days
but we are limited by measure
though seas they will remain always.

Cape Cod in '93
Christopher Black

We walked along the sea swept sands,
And so breathed the air from far-off lands,
We felt the world was in our hands,
For we were young and full of pride.
The world was then to us a place
Where shone the eyes of Nature's face,
Where making love was natural grace,
And no one had yet died.

We walked the dunes and watched a whale
That rolled dark back and belly pale,

Then smashed the waves, with fluking tail,
Upon a flowing tide,

And watched white sails on waters deep,
That raced on past the lighthouse keep,
Happy in each plunge and leap,
Like dolphins side by side,

While scudding clouds passed overhead
And pebbles glimmered gold and red,
As if they from the waters bled,
To lay there side by side,
Until we reached a beach-rose lane,
And as came down a gentle rain,
Did meet an old man with his cane,
Who stopped to step aside,

And next to him a lady stood,
A woman wise, as of the wood,

Who greeted us as well she could,
But for our future cried.

Twelfth Night
Safdar Bhatti

The resplendent moon of twelfth
A ravishing beauty clad
In bewitching sheen
Tinging the vast silent spheres
In the soothing haloes of
A prevailing, gentle lustre
Her spellbinding comeliness

That lucent silvery face
A divine enchantment
Instils in the rapt beholder
Passionate love of loves
And in the dreaming eyes
Sedative glory of gentle shine

Reminding me the goddess
Fell warmly in secret love
With the Latmian Shepherd

Stretched on a rustic bedstead
The visionary watches unwinking
"Phoebe and Endymion"
A film of profound passion
Enacted on the verdant summit
Of ancient Latmos
Longer agone

The spell cradles him to sleep
And lo, in the dreams
He finds him guised
In the semblance of Endymion

Odysseus's Feast from Homer
Ralston Purina

"As in the past then, no hesitation for a guest—
see to a ship and crew, loop oars to the tholes,
come back to the house to eat. In the main hall
order the elders gather—call the blind poet."
They hauled the black ship down, rigged the mast and spar,
oars in rawhide trailing, hoisted to test the white sail,
moored and retired to supper, the rooms and halls filled with men
of every age, women and girls within.
Sheep, boars, oxen all flayed apart,
gutted for the feast. The man of song,
cherished by the mixed blessings of the Muse,
knew the good and evil of life in blindness.
In a studded chair, wedged fast by a pillar,
they led his hands to the strings, nearby bread and wine.
For their part they heroically prepared their hearing,
then each man's hand went out upon the food.

Say My Name
Jennifer Torvalson

Say my name as the sea
with hushed sighs,
flowing caresses,
ebbing tides;

with fervent thunder
in tempests' throes,
echoing whist
torrid waves roil;

with hypnotic murmurs,
amid storm's aftermath—
serene whispers
'midst tranquil breaths.

Creativity
Rupa Rao

Pitted against machine
Human creativity is struggling
Inked by human or robot
Difference oft not caught
A verse is creativity's creation
Waxes emotions, thoughts fraught
Poetry machine — summoned, garnered of data filtered
Picks feelings deemed fit, man-made automaton vomits
How does a mere human better aeons of expertise
Sorted gems, select pieces, superior in flow in finesse
Make peace, none can run
Accept it, none can hide
AI is a wave to ride, create, to verse
AI is here to stay; like, love, dislike its way

Shower Refrain
Joel Aparecio Bernasor

Falling rain in the monsoon season
Like a stream's continuous falling
Which creates a refrain in frisson
Like a sweet melody in raining,
A refreshing drizzle coming down
From afar sky to the thirsty land
Raindrops like a melody sans shown
Within the beauty unveiled in wand,
As shower refrain let the rain brings
To horizon light of graceful day
As the mizzle brought us good tidings
With life flourishing along this way,
Great moments flurry tempo season
Such raindrops cadence point racing down
Pacing of the horizon which brings
Blessing to Creation's ascending midst

Wrap You in My Arms
Sarfraz Ahmed

You're a delicate flower
A rare find
I can feel you dissolve
Through my heart and mind
Like ecstasy
A drug that I can't get enough of
You're an addiction that I love.
You've got me on the cusp
Of pleasure and pain
I want to taste you again and again
You want me to surrender
Wrap you in my arms
Let you flutter through me
Like a butterfly in spring.
I want to give you my heart
I want to give you everything.

When Sincerity Meets Serenity
Sarah Tillbrook Wheatley

When sincerity meets serenity
The conscience calls for clarity
The enemy of brevity
Is formed in the disparity
Of all that is and hopes to be
In search of impartiality
We dream of the concordancy
Between our own imagery
And truth within reality
We are not what we want to see.

Nightfall
Emediong Asuquo

The sun slowly descends,
Down and down it goes into the sea,
The soft wind blows as the sky becomes dim,
Slowly and gradually the moon appears.

The owl on the old oak tree hooting,
The hunter's dog barking at shadows unseen,
The frogs in a nearby pond croaking,
Each disturbing the peace of the cold silent night.

Night hunters gathered and prepare,
Loading their rifles, fastening their hunters' torch,
Taking their hunters' bag and little companion,
They find their way into the thick dark bushes.

Night fishermen mend their net hurriedly,
The hook, rod and sinker all in place,
Wearing their big hat and fastening their torch,
They row up and down the sea for some catch.

The villagers lay motionless on their spread mat,
Snoring and snoring they drift to the dream world,
Nursing mothers singing a lullaby,
luring their babies to sleep,
To rest from the hard day's work.

The soft and cold breeze blew,
The villagers snuggle and lay peacefully,
With loincloth tied to the waist and blankets
tucked in round their bodies,
The village rings with snoring,
snuffling and silent breaths.

The Wind
Mike Rose

Late at night
I always listen to the wind
She sings me a love song
Tells me where she's been

She brings me stories
Of faraway places
And paints me pictures
Of all the beautiful faces

Some nights she whispers
Other nights she's loud
And I can hear her laughing
When she hides behind a cloud

I sit here under the stars
Trying to write some rhymes
While she plays beautiful music
On those old silver chimes

Then before I know it
She's gone without a warning
That's when I call it a night
So early in the morning

When I lay my head down
And finally close my eyes
I'll have that same old dream
Of her dancing across the skies

Gravel
Imelda Zapata Garcia

pebbles fill her mystic vision
runes , strewn on soiled ground
pulls them lose from tragic tendrils
polishes some to radiant beams
lifts them to heights she saunters
swearing her loyalty profound
for in her heart, they've cut the seams

a powerful voice does carry
pockets of rubble fit for scrubs
with her words, raises bubbles
makes velvet purses
from ears of sows
toughens her gentle touch
while edges of rocks she rubs
slicing her heart each time
a hardened heart takes her vows

she collects these bags of gravel
promising to lift them high
piles on the worn out shoulders
these massive invasive boulders
and slowly the weight will travel
dragging her soul from the sky

An Undaunted Woman
Phuntsho Wangchuk

A woman is a lotus whose fragrance
From the heaven to the earth cascades
To cater grains of love and endurance,
And whose virtuous colour never fades
Although in the sea of pain she wades.
She sows every seed of joy and peace
Even in the season of chaos and plight;
Her inborn kindness does never cease,
And in the darkness of moonless night,
Through her divine eyes, she finds light.
She may fall and she may sink in grief,
But by morrow she will rise like a dawn
To warm the day, and in a time so brief,
She will have herself to the bliss drawn
Despite her failure, despite woebegone.
As the bastion of love, harbinger of joy,
She counts the sunshine, not the storm;
She's the symbol of peace, God's envoy!
Deputed from above to heal and reform
Dilapidated souls as the universal mom.
You're a paragon of all, my dear mother!
You burn all your cells in your life-span
To warm us; and out of pain and bother,
You give us bliss, surpassing every man;
Thus I call you an undaunted woman.

Shades of Life
Joel Aparecio Bernasor

Aura of life been glimpse
Shades changes as duress
Red utter love express
Orange noted success
Yellow show happiness
Green shall reveal freshness
Blue denote trust such press
Pink sincerity bless
Purple voice dream caress,
Brown trustworthy assess
Black formality jess
White honesty selfless,
Vibrancies in life intricate
As emotions prevail sulcate
Rose to brick exhibit, pulsate
Mulberry to eggplant vibrate
Abalone to trout emanate
Forest to Kelly animate
Apricot to Dijon inflate
Apple to mahogany fate
Mellow to cyber corporate
Space to Prussian amalgamate
Cedar to umber qualitate
Animation dynamic rate

Solitude
Phuntsho Wangchuk

When the whole world does rotate
By the sweeping changes of time
And life rolls on the wheel of fate,
You esteem me as your most prime
And make our kinship high sublime.
Night swallows day, lies fake truth;
Evils destroy God, love ruins in lust;
But my friend, with brimless ruth!
You never bechance me to mistrust
And never let our friendship rust.
Whether I rise or fall, wake or sleep
You're always there with me indeed
From tip of joy till my sorrows deep
And till depth of my heart you read
To feel its pain and to see me bleed.
My bosom friend! My dear Solitude!
How kind you're to dress me in pride
And bless me with rays of fortitude!
Down the sea of loneliness, you guide
And lead me like your wedded bride.
I'm solitary; so they call me a loner;
But I tell them that I have a friend —
Mr. Solitude: my only lifelong owner
Who never discards me in any trend
Rather, escorts me till my life-end.

Hopeless
Kieran R. Eldritch

In shadows deep, two figures stand alone,
Silent companionship in a world turned to stone.
Each step heavier, the weight of chains unseen,
In their united descent, where hope has never been.

Beneath a sky void of stars they tread,
Walking hand in hand, to where even angels fear to tread.
The world around, an unrelenting grey,
Together they journey, with no dawn to light their way.

One whispers of solidarity, an anchor in the storm,
While the other's call promises release from form.
In the hushed void, where no light dares reside,
Together they embrace the inexorable slide.

United in desolation, their path set,
Bound by hope's absence, a fate they've met.

A Season of the Gift of the Old to the New
Bernie Martin

Apples of many hues, some having given up,
lost their grip, fallen to the ground.
Under layers of leaves sculpted by the wind
into a sort of burial mound.
Trees turning into transient autumnal beacons
of light backlit by the setting sun.
Up in the denuding branches birds' nests
and candyfloss mistletoe have been spun.
Mists that linger long into the day,
clear then return in a crepuscular gloom.
Nature starts its passage into hibernation
like it's going back to the womb.

Damaged Butterfly
Charlene Phare

Peel back the wings from this damaged butterfly
What's behind those eyes that you don't see cry
You just watch as she soars swiftly in the air
Wondering if she knows not everyone cares
Battles fought, wearing her scars with pride
Never reaching her potential, but she'll try
Grown up fast from a little caterpillar
Refusing to be consumed with pain killers
Fun loving tattooed through her deepest veins
Unable to be held back by her reins
Fluttering over the corn in the fields
Determined one day to be truly healed
Peel back the wings from this damaged butterfly
Passion replaced the tears, as they ran dry
She flies higher soaking up the atmosphere
With stealth and once again showing no fear
The world is full of problems, all wings break
Life is for living; there's no second retake

My Forever Senorita
Hahona Pita Batt

My forever senorita
The surety of your love
espouses salvation to my heart
Thine betrothen temple
in preordained eucharist covenant

Your espalier braided tresses
crown your aura in divinity
Your carapace parchment my
biblical Nirvana
My resplendent senorita cathedral
& chapel of adoration

Asomatous genesis of life
in pious intercede
My belfry spire stands proud
beseeching our conjugal betrothal

Your ambrosial aura
evangelises my heart
Baptised in the font of your eyes
Heaven's sacrament
spelunks my deepest resolve

Tumescent apertures feast & purchase
upon the communion of you
Goosebump parishioners titillate
embosomed globes

Salacious psalms
aroused in nubile petalled fold
Atop these penitent forms
our corporal vestibules
writhe in cathartic lust

Wanton catatonia
in onomatopoeic
crescendo of love
An urgency to break bread
& libate of your essence
as rosary beads of love cajole
in sensual secretion reverberate

The weight of our anointment
dimples bone
Moist laden tithes
seminally placate
as choirs erupt
in liturgical precipitate
Heavenly engorged in
life affirming
somatic exhale

Our Forgotten Place
Octobias Octobie Mashigo

There peace is still stealing thee
  Center stage at the still of the
    night,
  Breaking oppressors rules,
   Taking no hostages or haters
    Advises,
     Everyone is free to breathe
      Freely like an ocean,

   Mockers are walkers of the
    Road to freedom,
     Saw beauty at our palace
    They want to live peaceful life there
     And rock with us in our return
      To the forgotten palace,

Where golden laces are pages still
  Holding our stories that
   History was willing to tell our people,
Before you let lust kidnapped you
   Tile our palace with tears of sadness,

Let's forgive and forget
  Move on together with our people,
   Lead them and guide them to the
   Land of milk and honey,
  Coz in us they are seeing their
   Dreams fulfilled on future sheets

Heavenly Abode
Janet Stoyel

Those towering spires of argent stone
Adorned with dripping carved relief
Squinting eyes reach ever upwards
To cupola crowned in Verdigris blued,
Little more than paradisal avian roosts
Where birds wheel on unholy wings.
From catacomb halls in mouldering deeps
Pilgrim feet raise miasmic clouds,
Intimate sanctified dust of ages past.
Resurrected mediaeval old, lost souls
Entombed in blown-glass Manga style,
Stained, painted, eternally corseted in lead.
Built to last an eternity, heavenly edifices,
Awesome, inspirational places of worship.
Roses trampled along visionary labyrinths,
Devotees seeking the way, the truth, the light
Traversing basilica, colonnade, and apse
Worshippers, gawkers, searching, seeking.
All the while, outside mists lift, disperse,
Become tears from heaven—holy rain,
Encouraging secular mis-fits to shelter,

Find succour in the welcoming arms
Of an olden monumental multiplex
Giving generously in senescence age.

Insomniac Poet
Sarfraz Ahmed

Too many pills
Can blur the imagination
Can stir the pot
Make you hot
Words begin to rot
Begin to repeat
Between the sheets.
While the world sleeps
Nice and tight
Words continue to bite
Thoughts flourish
Make you think
Burn through the ink
Sleep is denied
For the insomniac poet
Who aches inside
Every second
Every moment
Words collide and break
For the insomniac poet
Suffering wide awake.

Delayed Reaction
Charlene Phare

Senses hit out of the blue
Something said, yet nothing new
Slowly thoughts penetrate
Second class fuse, feeling irate

Somehow the words have pierced my skin
So I must shut them out, not let them in
Speak to my soul to comfort me
Shock to the system drastically

Somewhere deep down trouble was caused
Sometimes our lives are paused
Seeking subtraction
Suffering from delayed reaction

Silently we will recover
Slow burning flames we can smother
Swamped in self-love constantly
Showing resistance

Dam the Dawn
Steven Elliott Borodkin

Dam the dawn, its covenant.
I who worship the fickle fame of neon.
Urban.
It paints the night with impression.
A memorandum. An implication of loneliness.
dark illumination, cavorting.
Vampire, I feed on its delicate facility.
Straining at its tenor.
I take cover in its pallet, seamless hues, pedestrian makeup.
My footsteps annoy the trash, as it scurries away to hide
from the broom.
Sensual, a forest of colored doorways, shuttered storefronts.
Sentinel, garrison of its bones and borders, of its residence.
Not one soul shall pass under your ambient glow.
You are mine.

Rain
Selena Ou

I love this calm and silent rain
in England's summer afternoon,
Consistent and consolable.
Its gentle pouring touches all,
Feeding the thirsty and
making life more lively.
Its soft fingers soothe creased minds,
eliminating dusts on thoughts;
Trouble hearts made to feel easier,
like a breeze through timeless mountains,
free and meditative.

Yet all this was given
with no single pompousness,
Only the pure purity of
a summer afternoon rain.

Orbiting Questions
Deepali Parmar

I have walked
upon fallen leaves,
heard them crackle under one step
and then took another—
I was hoping to be heard
this way, sincerely.
They came, tried to look at me
and struck me down for
being tall.
It goes on in the name
Of something shapeless like love,
country or life.
Don't stop me from
Lifting a pencil to draw
this face.
It holds a familiar shape.
You tried to be 'there'
Without trying to go away—
away into—your desire-slummed heart,
into your eager munificence,
and off course, the stream you want to be
with a rock in your hand. Huh!
How many times should this head look up?
Will not the sun shine upon me?

I too need the yellowing.
How many times should this circle spin?
If it's round
Shouldn't it be complete?

I Wish I Could Fly
Richard Harvey

There are times in my life that I wish I could fly
Way over the hilltops so high in the sky
To the land that I dream of, to the land that's my home
To my friends and my loved ones to the love I have known

We could sit by the water; it would be such a thrill
We could hold hands together and walk up the Big Hill
We could sit in the treehouse; we could drink from the stream
We could share with one another all our hopes and our dreams

There are times in my life that I wish I could forever see
All the potential, all the beauty that lies within you and me
The heart that is beating, the breath of life that's inside you
The soul that is yearning to do all those great things too

We could join hands together, and away we would fly
Way over the hilltops so high in the sky
Share our hopes and our dreams, our hurts and pain
Take a drink from the cup and never be the same again

There are times in my life that I wish I could fly
Way over the hilltops so high in the sky
I would soar right to your house and knock upon the door
When you answered, I'd hug you like I never have before

We could sit out by the water; it would be such a thrill
We could hold hands together take a walk up the hill
We could sit and have a coffee or drink from a stream
We could share with one another all our hopes and our dreams

Into the Dark
Terry Bridges

This thin bare tapestry of dusk
Fading light scatters across the grass
Ask nothing of immeasurable night
At the winding-down of daily tasks
The owl of Minerva hoots a welcome
To the sleepless creations of restless minds
Horror fascination excitement all comes to this
One person's nightmare is another's bliss
Separate moments possess distinct different fates
Evaporate like dew-drops in watery moonlight
The black fractured silent hours await

A Home in the Hills
Andy Allen

A wind blows through the valley
And follows the River Calder
Channelled by ancient hills of green.
It whispers tales
Of millennia of drama
In the wake of which
The mountains stand stoic. Heroic.

Only buildings of stone
Will weather this landscape,
As hardy as those who dwell in them,
And as unshakeable as the community
That made its home here.

Far in the distance Stands Stoodley Pike;
A symbol of resilience and craft.
It tells the wind to turn around
And go tell those stories again.

I Remember Bluebells
Christopher Black

I remember bluebells,
Soft, strewn among the trees,
And I remember songbirds,
And running by the sea,
And I remember one long night,
You took your leave of me.

You took your leave, without a word,
'Midst shadows of the night
Hands outstretched to take you back,
You slipped beyond my sight,
And the only softening sound I heard
Above my falling tear,
Was the distant sound of nature's love,
In a cricket's song of cheer.

I remember bluebells,
Like stars among the dew,
And I remember mists of rain,

And all my words spoke true,
But aye, you wanted someone else,
And all my words were vain,
As you took from me the rose you gave,
Another's heart to gain.

How To Fulfil Dreams
Shakat Aziz Hajam

How to fulfil dreams there
Where one often takes breath in the net of fear
of disappearance and of death
And one carries more coffins but palanquins, few.

Not many raiments for weddings
But more coffins one has to sew.
How to fulfil dreams there
Where each moment is spent in jails and yowls
And youths decay in dingy jails.
Where one while fishing, fishes out a corpse
Of a mother's only progeny and succour
Beheaded or mutilated or putrefied
Or still from his wounds is dripping blood of innocence.
How to fulfil dreams there
Where one's childhood is caged, divested of its joys
Where deranged mothers (as if their sons)
are lullabying toys.

Summer Storms
Lynne Truslove

Rain caressing my cheeks
A gentle breeze whipping my dress
Gulls squawking, circling the skies
Swooping for prey
Waves lapping the shores
Clouds gathering speed
Darkening the view
A chill rips through my clothes
As the trees begin to come alive
Awakened rudely from their sweet slumber
The crackle in the air
Gaining momentum
Lighting flashing seconds behind
Electrical static, filling my surroundings
As I gaze in wonderment
Birds take shelter but highly vocal
Mankind following their lead
As I follow my path
Undeterred by the storm brewing
Enjoying the true peace around me

Touched
Michael Balner

I close my eyes
and I disappear
in shouts of seagulls,
gibberish of people,
and the roaring of engines.

A warm soft palm is touching
my face,
the same way
you did —   the evening sun.
Mellow wind is gently blowing
through my hair,
the same way
your fingers used to run.

And I melt into those sounds,
and I lean into that palm,
and I rest in all those feelings,
just for a little while.
I don't want to leave here,
but I spread my wings and I take off
                — to the sky.

This
            is a good spot to be,
I suppose, more often, I should come,
I could hardly choose
      a better place
and a better time —

I am,
right here,
right now.

Lightning Bugs
Manolo Piquero

Stepped out into the muggy, end of June night.
Recent thunderstorm gave no relief from the heat.
But in the air, as if the stars came down to greet me,
small yellow glows, blinking their light on and off
in rhythmic sways through the dusky night.
Appeared they were lighting my path
as I slowly walked in the dark.
Keeping beat with their hearts,
each step would reveal more small stars

blinking into existence in front of me,
while slowly disappearing
as their light extinguished momentarily.
With the moon too ashamed
to show itself this evening,
glow from these marvels from nature,
was a welcome surprise
as they did their evening dance
looking for their perfect mate.
How wonderful it would be
to never be afraid of the dark,
everywhere you went, carried your own light.
For only short seconds at a time
would you have to remain in the dark,
before the light inside you would show you the way.
Way a lighthouse's beacon lit the way at night,
to find a similar soul in the vast blackness.
I can see why children would want to capture
their own blinking star and keep it in a jar.
To hold a bit of heaven and
glimpse upon its simple beauty
makes the night a less scary place.

A South African Sunrise
Bernie Martin

God paints a different picture
every morning.
The icy blue pastel of the sky,
nature adorning
the scene with shafts of sunlight
shaped by the trees.
Cotton wool clouds keep their distance,
approach the sun with unease
like, if they were to block any part
it would be a sin.
The low sun creates a landscape of shadows
that holds within
the messages God sends down to us.
Transient pictures that fade.
Everything will be different tomorrow.
Perfection portrayed.

Momma's Boy
Jack H. DeKnight Jr

Years ago I had a dream
Of flying big machines
and loving many hearts
and stopping war before it starts
Years ago you called me momma
from the porch and in for dinner
Had the world wrapped in your arms
Every day I was a winner
Hop a train here with me now
to a time we wake up beaming
Yesterday is dead and gone
Only for the ones that are not dreaming

A Love Story
Sushma Sharma

I have never pined for you
Didn't look in the nooks and corners of life
Or scratch the wounds just to experience the blood
I went along in life ...unmindful
But as night enveloped me
your presence came alive
Under the stars and a bright moon
The waves of the ocean
Reminded me of the times
We chased the clouds
And watched the sunset together
Sipping life's moments
Incredible conversations
Never-ending words
Creating poems sitting in a bus line by line
The metaphors and imagery
So vivid
Conveying the sense of urgency
Sharing laughter and millions of cups of tea,
Walking barefoot on the beach and the roads
with no thought for tomorrow.
Zillion feelings turning my inside out
Denying those feelings
Yet holding them tenderly in our hands
Asif holding tenderness itself tenderly
Delicate moments demanding truth
Yet we walked together
Sometimes for real or imaginary
Like the fleeting moments
Letting go and holding freshness
in the palms of our hands
We grew up together ...
An invisible bond only to feel.
I called this love and friendship
in my utter foolishness.
It was soul retrieval ...

A Toy
Simon Drake

I want to watch the lights go out
When I look into your eyes
Wanting to be the last thing you ever see
Knowing you're someone I despise

You thought you'd gotten away with it
As the final credits rolled
No my love, you're not so lucky
I'm here to take your soul

Decades since you've seen my face
I was only a little a boy
Young and confused, a child abused
Your plaything, just a toy

Now the calf has become a bull
Oh, how the tables turned
You, fuelled my rage and hatred
I was well and truly burned

No one would ever believe my story
All the things you did to me
Just our little secret Mum
Kept within the family

For years, I wish I'd killed you both
With my own bare hands
Now a registered lethal weapon
With intent and murderous plans

Some days I think I've gotten over you
Then I get hit in waves
You should've been jailed for what you did
I wasn't a son, I was your slave

33 years and still counting
Thinking of what I should've said and done
Instead, patiently I wait in silence
My mind's a loaded gun

Absence of Belonging
Jennifer Torvalson

She found belonging in its absence—
amid other lost, abandoned things;
with shards of broken sea glass
and feathers shed from soaring wings;
with missing pages from oft-read books
and trinkets that no longer shine—
she is kin to forgotten spaces,
the overlooked and
left behind.

Untitled
Deepali Parmar

Held between the bittersweet
Grip of mud-palms
Chiselling a moment in time
Mould me into a shape that calms.
Swallowed and spilling
at once eaten
yet held by
the moans slipping out
of midnight's lips
to kiss each star
and burst into
the eternity called "us".

Puzzle my senses and destroy
my flow again,
angled, this way into you—
What do I care, what I know,
where I go…

DaysNight
Sarah Tillbrook Wheatley

As sun of day, day turns to moon of night
He says, it's your turn to light the skies
Fill the world with lullabies
And with sweet surrendered sighs
All is right, all is fine
As soft beds release the minds
And their consciousness combine
With the images behind
It was illusive for dark time
Now the meaning is imbibed
And they bid the past goodbye
With the understanding why
As the sun of day turns from moon of night
And they see that all's all right

Cabbage Patch Agony
Neil Mason

Here I grow in the roughest part of the garden
Where even the toughest of weeds go around in pairs,
armed with sawn off hosepipes
Stones, stones and more stones is my growing room
While carrots and onions live in fine soil palaces
I also have to put up with the neighbour's kids' football
I get a lot of heading practice
Maybe I'll get picked for England
Scoring the winning goal at Wembley with a diving header
But I'm stuck here in a cabbage patch agony
Put me on the transfer list
This is hardly the Savoy

The Crescent Moon Bear
Deepali Parmar

The polar bear floated
Swallowing a sliced moon
Spitting the crescent at the dark
Swelling to meet a white eye
The night goes unblinking
Watch your oars slipping and
Sinking:

The polar bear floats
Calls you uphill, uphill
You walk and walk
Till you learn to be still
Swallow his moon
Slice your pride
Look up at the dark and spit
Don't wipe your face
the drop
That will help you sink
Slip out the other side
Swell under your skin
Float with the bear upon your
Brow.
Turn your dark eye —
white

Where others saw Chaos, I saw Patterns
Patrick Darnell

I've lived in this little house ten years
Near the floodplain of the des Plaines River
The soil around here is black gold
Everything grows and thrives
Hostas and daffodils bloom in winter's thaw
Four season indigenous crab-apple trees,
Boxwood shrubs, river bottom vines,
Confuse city folks.

Snow melting drenches the soil
And earthworms angle up to surfaces
An old friend shows up at that moment
And feasts on juicy worms
I call him old friend.
He and a few others were here
My first year
And returned every spring since.

His red breast after ten years is not smooth
The feathers are dishevelled
I suppose from migrations
To where it's less cold he has travelled
He chirps, hops, spies, and pecks,
And is comfortable with me.
He is unforgettable, and noble
He is King Robin on my street.

Evening
D. A. Simpson

Evening shadows fell
wafting through the mist of night-tide
whispering to the trees
of mysteries unknowable
spun in a world of dreams
An opaque realm
veiled in shades of purple
shrouded in a haze of dusky blue

Where a mellow glow of ivory
emitted by the orb of night
seeped through the obscurity
weaving a path through the silent land

As an ethereal lambency
emerged from another reality
issued by a waning moon

While the hour of night
exulted upon high
in the infinite firmament
Lowering a canopy of indigo
onto the slumbering dominion below,
the unfathomable darkness
engulfing an infinite celestial canvas

Cuddle Up
Bernie Martin

It's many
years ago
now.

Cuddled up
like we're on the
bough

of a special tree
in some magical
place,

far away from
the rest of the human
race.

We knew only
one feeling,
love

and you fit me
like a perfect, matching
glove.

We Are The Invisible
Christopher Black

We are the invisible,
The unseen, the unheard

You know us, by our shadows,
Cast in dark rooms,
By a cigarette's glow,
Or the sound of our steps,
On an empty street,
Reflections in the sun,
Whispers in the wind,
You know us by our sweat,
You know us by our tears,
Pouring like oil,
Glistening like pearls,
By our songs and laments,
By our heads turned away,
You know us by our hopes,
Imprisoned in the cloth,
The plastic, the steel,

All the things, those others use,
By our poverty, bred of riches,
By our unpaid bills,
Our sleepless nights,
Our hollow days,
Our worn-out shoes.

Body, Mind, Spirit
Shirley Rose

I crave your corporeal
How yours intertwines with mine
We fit from our fingers to our toes
And everything in between

I celebrate your cerebral
Our lofty thoughts and dreams
Rise like incense smoke
In the heights of a cathedral

I enjoy your ethereal
And, God forgive me,
I envy it too
You seem softer, quieter,
closer to Heaven
Than I ever hope to

Body, mind, spirit
The true trifecta of a human
And lucky we who in our Oneness
Can become a Twoness,
and create a Trinity

Grey is Great
Selena Ou

When the coldness
slaughters the greenery,
even a rose's final bud,
tilted and dropped dead,
I want grey —
Grey grass,
Grey sky,
Grey air and
Grey self.

Arrogance turned the tender heart
into pale mince,
I want grey to seal the wound,
the bleeding, and sooth
the pain.

Standing against a cruel invasion,
I want grey,
that kind of thick grey frog
wrapping the castle of mind
Like mediaeval soldiers
guard their kingdoms.

Grey is peace,
Grey is luxury,
Grey is eternity,
If I have to lose all others.

Little Funerals
Kelli Walker

we bury the remnants
of the things we've lost
as if covering the tracks
of existence will somehow
relieve us
of the memory of what was
and we dig,
and we mask it,
in shrouds and in caskets
and we are forever attending
a succession
of little funerals

All Set
Jack H. DeKnight Jr

How long can I stare
up at the blue sky and think
without selling my soul
to the paper and ink
without dancing with devils
or painting lines red
how long till my heart
is very well fed
What is this magic
a gaze in the air
I am discovering things
not really there
and I ponder, I worry,
I sweat and I stink
All for the love of these words
Set in ink

Red Bud
Sherry Healy

A black rose petal
Falling from a withered stem
A red bud remains

A table awaits
An empty flask of wine sits
Waiting a soon end

No longer will the scents speak
A bewildered petal rest

A lost love aware
A romance has come to end
Grieving their affair

It seems nothing lasts
A summer time ends too fast
A red bud remains

Summer has come to an end
A red bud will come again

Turn Around
David Knauss

You patiently await that baby girl or boy
Filled with wonder, love, a parent's joy
You turn around and they're walking
Turn around and now they're talking
You turn around and you're chasing them
Through stores trying to reel them in
You turn around and they're in school
Though the way some act school seems cruel
You turn around and they're on a Senior Prom date
Though you'd acted as if you couldn't wait
In reality it is like a piece of your own heart
Just went for a walk in the dark
You turn around and college has come to graduation
You celebrate with a lot of elation
Then you turn around as you watch them getting wed
Then turn around as the cycle is renewed
Each turn in life has a glory of its own
As you see them grown with kids now growing
A wonderful process that can astound
As at each step we get turned around

This Day Like Others Dreaded in Hope
Kwaku Adjei Fobi

In the interim
between the long cast umbra
and the sliver of a halo,
I push a prayer,
not loud, not screamed in anger at the Lord.
Just a little whimper filled with laud.

On this day,
like others dreaded in hope,
I am celled in my chamber
like a jailbird.
Daring no flight.
The entire earth is cast into a jail
marked by masks.
I can feel you, hide and hair,
your thinking head in the closet
and your errant feet
stepping on our conscience,
making distance,
not progress.

Summer's Splendor
Manolo Piquero

Scent of freshly cut Kentucky Blue
lingers in the gentle breeze.
Choosing a shady spot for our blanket, lying down,
I peer up at her; as the sunlight twinkling through trees
Silhouetted by her auburn hair, gives her a heavenly aura.
Rustling of leaves provides a soothing song for our picnic,
where nothing matters right now,
but being here with her.
Playfully pull her down beside me,
our fingers greedily entwine.
We watch a solitary cloud,
lost in a vast sea of azul celeste.

Wispy taffy pulled and shaped,
appearing as a Chinese dragon twisting,
turning its serpentine coils, disappearing
out of sight behind the old oak.
Turn away from the nebulous cinema;
Find her intensely watching me
with hands on chin and emerald gaze.
Cheeks turn crimson from being observed.
I return the gesture and admire her in supine position.

She doesn't turn from my scrutiny,
instead, enjoys the attention.
Mind drinking in all of the beauty before me;
Strand of hair refusing to stay behind her ear,
floral summer dress rippling in the wind,
touch of her warm alabaster skin,
sound of her laughter, a glorious chorus.
Vision of summer's splendor,
the hopes and the dreams.
Opening doors long shut tight!
Gloom of winters past, a distant memory.

A Song of Light and Dark
D. R. Parsons

Heed the words of this dark song,
A forewarning made to all.
For all who remain in a place too long,
Consider the ancient wall.
Once was sturdy, once was strong,
Now crumbles, fit to fall.

The builder who, now long gone,
Proud of his endeavour.
A marvel raised where it belonged,
Built to last forever.
Lost now to an age bygone,
The curse of time and weather.

Heed the words of this dark song,
Heed a warning call.
Wither the ones, who won't move on,
Corrosion eats them all.
For those who remain in a place too long,
Will crumble like old walls.

Rejoice the words, a song of light,
A spark can set you free.
For those who leave the dull for bright,
Consider the birds in trees.
From their perch, from great height,
Imagine what they see.

Many the bird, delight in flight,
Proud, their wings of feather.
A marvel soars, by day and by night,
Looks down on fields of heather.
Free are their minds, free is their sight,
When free, the bonds that tether.

Rejoice the words, a song of light,
These words to help you see.
That as the birds, enjoying flight,
So could you and me.
For those who leave the dull for bright,
Forever will be free.

Panorama of Surprise
Geoff Stockton

Take me where the watery expanse meets the sky,
a horizon display of silhouetted trees awry
Let's go and witness the panorama of surprise,
a variable blend of Irish lake-land's azure blue skies.

Dip a hand in the darker waters of this Irish Lake
and feel the earthy energy you wish to partake.
Holding on tight to its ceaseless sway,
slipping through our fingertips on this showery day.

Hear that melody, the rhythm of the waves,
as they chuckle across our pushing bows
Rhythmic crashes, and splashes too,
listen with me, tell me do what you hear that's new?

Let this music carry us ever forward
to explore the waters with no worries or fuss.

The notes sing out loud in the warming breeze,
travel far and wide, with such joy and ease.
Ponder and feel the endless reach of Lough Erne
Its secrets lie dormant, biding time to be.

Unfathomable depths, mysteries await,
as we moored there in such a privileged state.

I Will Change History
Jacob Daniel Laari

I grew up in homes where fishes dwell in a pool of sand
I grew up in homes where trees cry for shades
I grew up in homes where mountains are shorter than rocks
I grew up in homes where dogs chew metals as bones.
I will change history
They walked but I will run
They drank from gourds but I will drink from
The lion's skull
They fought with spears but I will fight with arrows
They took the smooth path but I will follow
The rough path.
I will change history
For I know the moon moves slowly but by
Daybreak it crosses the sky
And when a monkey learns to jump
From tree to tree, it never falls.
I will change history.

Gallant Poet
Jannetta Lamort

In my mind's eye,
a garden of silent statues stand
as effigies to his love and idealism —
evocative tellings in poetic form
— timestamps marking his past

Until…
In Requiem

In my mind's eye,
a gallant poetical figure tilts
in the mire of our abandoned garden —
I caress his clay feet and marvel
how his painted brilliance fades
— under a retrospective gaze

Today
Rhiannon Owens

Today, I felt the breeze through my hair
Whispering in my eager ear,
Running soft fingers down the back of my neck
Stroking my flushed cheeks,

Today, I saw the leafy green before me
I saw a place I'd always know,
I breathed and my lungs were light
There were fields, trees... I weep,

I weep because...
Today, I saw your face in the sky,
The clouds were turning ominous
but my horizon was blue, my horizon bright...

Today, I saw the beauty to which I'd been blind
Today, I saw that everything was alright,

Today, I saw
I saw
You...

I saw
That for all
I have lost,

In you... I can find

My Darling Boy
Gregory Richard Barden

oh ... have you seen my darling boy
blond hair, like corn silk, falling?
lost, his sparkling absinthe eyes
but still, my heart keeps calling

I thought I saw him run away
with a young girl, hand-in-hand
swallowed by the ocean mist
their footprints in the sand

oh, have you seen my darling boy
with a smile broad and bright?
seems he went a-wandering
in a full moon, late one night

while captured by his fancies
he's inclined to court a whim
so counting evening fireflies
would be grave concern for him

oh, have you seen my darling boy
with dreams and hopes anew?
he holds the mind to conquer
a kingdom, grand ... or two

and yet he'd rather spin you
tall tales that make you smile
wise anecdotes, adventurous
to charm you and beguile

oh, have you seen my darling boy
replete with loves and life?
he's apt to wink or tease
you suffused with virtue, rife

he's endeared to melancholy
yet he masks it with a laugh
his child's heart aches for others
but breaks on their behalf

oh, have you seen my darling boy?
he sings an impassioned tune
of swirling maelstroms, seas of suns
and the faces of the moon

he's oft to feign a scoundrel
though he's chivalrous and kind
and loves to search a sunken heart
for the treasure he may find

oh, have you seen my darling boy?
no — I doubt you ever will
as I call to him across the years
but the air is hushed and still

so, tho' I've chased him, wide and far
I'm quite sure I'll never see
his corn silk hair and absinthe eyes
for that darling boy

... was me.

Home
Kwaku Adjei Fobi

The dragnet of memoirs sag,
down the dancing dirt roads,
the gentle hum in the acacia —
music to my ears
amidst the road rage, din and catcalls
timbred by stress.

Towards the old homestead
I lose count of laboured steps,
hurried by waiting arms, waiting love

— Mama's....

cultured, heightened by time,
coiled into a courteous heart.
Paradise beats under her chest.

I will offer her
a bouquet of smiles,
long before and after collapsing
into a whining chair,
clutching a calabash of welcome,
smooth brown unwrinkled
unlike her journeyed skin.

I will wait for the brand new morn sky
to stoop over us both, to light up her face,
to launch my vast collections of city buzz.

All I Have
Andy Reay

There are many that say
You shouldn't live in the past
That the velvet covered warmth
of memories will prevent
passage to the future

Alas I see no future
only the increasing glow of pain, of angst
the only ray of light
comes from visions
dreams, and comfort from the past

I can sit alone and
quietly converse with those
who knew me well, who loved
and understood me
and were alive, in my past

There are many that say
You shouldn't live in the past
But once my joints are fused
and my lungs fail and
I can no longer communicate
Memories will be all I have

The Stranger
Emediong Asuquo

Kicking sand and dry leaves,
The stranger wanders round the town,
Hair as big as the lion's fur,
Nails as long as the leopard's claws.

Mumbling and murmuring the stranger strides,
Taking slow pace it continues its journey,
Wallowing in pains and regrets,
Cursing the day it was brought to earth.

Looking up at the sky, the heavens so high,
Dropping it head down, the earth so close,
Looking forward to it unending journey,
Wondering if it would ever have an end.

Tired and famished, the stranger lay on the path,
It feet could go no more far,
Closing it eyes and calling out to death,
Awaiting its departure from the cruel wicked world.

Opening it eyes, smiles crept to it face,
Standing up, feeling no more pains,
Walking round, beholding the beautiful sight,
Hearing the voice of its Creator it hurries home.

Bidding farewell to the once cruel world,
And taking it Creator's outstretched hand,
To the home it long awaited,
The home it will find peace eternal.

To Wait or Die
Pritha Lahiri

Theatre of the absurd played
I sang, danced and strayed
But you never came...
Under the leafless tree we sway
    My friend and I
Vacuous talks betray
Yet you never came...
Confounding thoughts linger
Senseless arguments bicker
Whimsical intrigues fray
Alas, you never came...
How long do we wait, Godot?
    My friend and I
The trees have sprouted few leaves
Your messenger yet lies
Am in Hamletian dilemma
To wait or die.

Talk to Me
Anna Obara

Talk to me
Ensnare me with words
until I run out of breath
tie my wrists
with exclamation marks
and drink from my mouth
voiced vowels
just talk to me
let dirty metaphors
vibrate with echo
hot syllables
stroking my thighs
let them burn
as I do
under the touch of your letters...

Love's Symphony
S. E. Toner

The wind softly touches the violin
Like a feather in the wind
Barely moving
Gently falling
Caressing the strings
So breathlessly
Endlessly
Searching
For paradise
Where every movement sings
Trailing on the breeze
Rescuing me
So helplessly
As time honours
Each note that's played
And I'm lost for days
Whilst the music just plays
Serenading
The love that's cherished
Within
Yearning
As my mind carries on
Learning
Touching tenderly
So gently
Like the wind
Plays the violin
In perfect harmony
Love's symphony
Cherished
Within.

Dig Me a Whole
Gemma Tansey

Burn my ashes and distance the near
Rip my clothes off and fondle the fear
Blow my soul and smoke my life
Devour my grief and slit with a knife
Sing my pain and silence my tune
Darken my sun and brighten my moon
Swallow my anger and choke on my air
Breathe my sin and singe my hair
Lick my wounds and sip my tears
Poke my eyes and deafen my ears
Touch my mind and stroke my control
Slap my emotion and move my goal
Kick my psyche and feel my heart
Stamp on my ego and bury the tart
Savour the flavour and spit me out
Hear my sight and taste my doubt
Smell my worry and paint my face
Feel my sorrow and eat my disgrace
Chew my heartbeat and weld my signs
Erase my memory and write the lines
Murder my joy and mould my hand
Feel my hunger and wrap me in sand
Suck my kisses and squash my desire
Torture my truth and comfort my liar
Shrink my brain and squeeze my soul
Pick me apart and dig me a whole

The Trader
Madhu Gangopadhyay

Mint kiss
Holding ephemeral love
In ruby lips;
She rides off into the sunset
To script another
Incomplete story!
She has mastered the art
Of enacting romance
And dwells in a world of fakery.
Found solace in ignominious misery!

Puffing swirls of smoky love
Susurration of promises!
Masquerading loyalty,
In mint kiss and powdered cheeks
The kohl eyes deceive
Romance!

Carting love in paper hearts;
Off into imaginary sunsets she rides:
As another deceptive moon arises,
To wrap her yearnings in dotted silver!

When the veil of darkness slips,
The copper sun and
The glistening coins on her palm tease!

And she plays the cursed Prometheus
Every single eve;
Resurrecting the intestines of love!

The Hazelnut and the Big Bang
Iain Strachan

It started with a Big creative Bang.
A hazelnut-sized universe was made
That held the seed of everything; it sprang,
And, pregnant with dark energy, was laid.

A tiny kernel: this was Everywhere.
This Bang resounded even where you sit
And every other place, both here and there
The fuse of Genesis was brightly lit.

An English mystic, fevered, saw the same:
A hazelnut, and wondered what it meant
"It's everything that's made", the answer came;
To make, sustain, contain, was Love's intent.

Thus, Julian of Norwich saw in part
How scientists today describe the Start.

It Teases Me
Madhu Gangopadhyay

I love my shadow
My twin so free
Appears and disappears
As it will be!
And I, a mortal fool
Tossed in existential whirlpool
Forever grappling with destiny
Chained to absurd societal rules
Enact clownish roles many!
And my shadow hiding its face,
Vanishes in darkness without a trace!
While I, every day,
Darker darkness embrace!
My wayward shadow regales
And I envy its artless grace!

A Restless Soul
Amelia Lynn

I was made for more

More late nights
and obscure books
midnight drives
with music that fills the void
of the tears I never learned to cry
more daytime dreams
feet on the ground
hand and hand
fighting for the voices that deserve
to be heard
new cities, different countries
an entire universe still to seek
the depths of conversation
in a language only we learned to speak
boots that collect dust
from more than just that corner in the room
the courage of wisdom
found in compassion
of our humanity
more dances in the dark
where the stars always remind me

I am home

I was made for more

A restless soul

Whirling Dervishes
Farha Abbasi

Whirl whirl whirl
To the melody of
unheard music
In realms of mysticism

Find the rhythm of love
Swirl in compassion
Seeking in zest
The path to the only truth
Ignoring blistered feet
Scorched by the heat
Of hatred, insincerity and ingratitude
A heart putrefied by
greed and worldly servitude

Mind shackled by unfulfilled desires
Soul imprisoned in the web of
pretence relations

Whirl whirl whirl
Harder, faster and in sync
With the universe
Round and round
hear the chains breaking

Taste the sweet freedom
Unleashed soaring energy
Rising to the final abode
Outro the final note is playing
rest your weary soul
In the bosom of eternity
To be reborn again someday

Between the Trees
Jade Wickens

It's getting hard to see the light between the trees,
Visions of memories begin to fade,
Although once stood a strong, tall mind,
Now seems to crumble over time,
As darkness begins to seep in slowly,
A way out is more difficult to find,
Happiness turns to black,
The warmth turns to cold,
All my senses are becoming blind,
I feel no pain, joy or sorrow,
No prayer, no longer hope for tomorrow,
The past so far set behind,
I see no future, no fight
As it's getting hard to see the light ...
Between the trees.

Restless
Jennifer Torvalson

Restless,
she is mercury confined;
imprisoned in a foreign realm,
fettered by iron fists of time.
Entrapped by a reality she wants no portion in,
she is tethered by circumstance
to a fate, grown wearisome.
Her gypsy-caravan soul is lost to dreams,
borne up on the waves of tears wept
for a life of might have-beens;
riding white horses
stirred up by the tides in their wake,
and crashing into forlorn shores
of happiness waylaid.

Fragments and Memories
Jacalyn Evone

The painting has darkened over time.
It has become old and worn.

Remembering the solitary
spaces of loneliness and
comforting reassurances

that it is OK to grieve loss
and mourn passings,
while yearning
for the fragments of
reminders of pleasant days
and hopefulness.

The reclaimed moments of joy
and times shared,
of faces filled with laughter.

Dreaming of the images in the painting
faded and darkened over time.

The ones that bring back memories
of laughter still heard and faces
still seen, coming through the door.

All the sadness discarded to leave sounds
of the good times that feel so very real.

A Stubborn Desire
Kwaku Adjei Fobi

You sowed a whim, reaped a whimper.
Over day's imprints cast in dew, hang,
bedazzling your infantile fancy,
your shallow lake of fiction.
I am trawling the joys apart
into the sunshine pulse.
The soft sprinkle of sanity,
something into which we can all soar
and feel showered with a stubborn desire,
a gripping prognosis beyond grief...
Wake charged, above the skyline,
over the nimbus,
the trembling scaffolds of tomorrow.
Wake favoured and flavoured,
above your doubts
beyond the snapping sharks
of momentum.

The End of the Road
Rafik Romdhani

Go till the end of the road like fire
but bargain not with one another.
We fall from our own trees one by one
like ripe fruits before ants and worms.
We fall like foreordained dreams
and stifled whispers to a wet sand.
Go till the end with the heavy suitcases
you hardly carry with both hands.
Go alone, leave everything outside
before you plunge deep down
with nothing more than life's cards
and worn out ribs to meet their end.

The Rain Lover
Pureheart Wolf

As the raindrops on the car window
Each little drop is unique and reflective
A day for a long drive,
With no particular destination.
The rain is cleansing,
I stop the car,
I find an inner calm, relaxing,
listening to the drops that
trickle down from the metal roof,
My mind hums in rhyme.

It takes me back to my childhood days
Sheltering below the leaves of big old trees.
Curled up snug with wellies and gloves.
A calmness flows through me
I am grounded and all is well
All the mistakes I have made in life
Don't worry me now,
Not at this time.

Not, while I am the storm's lover.
If only others could feel the love,
the whispers of each drop.
Then they would know that
getting wet is just the outer layer
Go beyond the superficial and feel each tear.
There you will find serenity.

A Sonnet to the Setting Sun
Safdar Bhatti

When Helios dwindles from here away
On the self-same hour it shines on Britain
Within me starts raging sombre foray
Of nostalgic throes, of heavier pain

My longing heart you waft away with thee
My eyes, the poorest exiles, gaze for long
Now bright now dim with dreaming ecstasy
And weltering hopes within the bosom throng

Darker shades of eventide sadly fall
Pelting heavily on the sullen breast
And cardiac effusions crying call
"O when with their hankered sights, eyes be blest?"

Abruptly heaves the bosom colder sighs
And briny dew glistens in yearning eyes

Sunset
Kehinde Dare

The angry air swirled
and eddied round
the ball of fire.
The battered cloud
regurgitated darkness
and the ravenous night
spreads her black blanket
across the earth, signalling
the end of the day.

WHEELSONG POETRY ANTHOLOGY 3

About Wheelsong Books

Wheelsong Books is an independent poetry publishing
company based in the ocean city of Plymouth,
on the beautiful Southwest coast of England.
Established by poet Steve Wheeler in 2019,
the company aims to promote previously unheard voices
and encourage new talent in poetry. Wheelsong is also
the home of the Absolutely Poetry anthology series,
featuring previously unpublished and emerging poets
from around the globe.

Wheelsong has more poetry publications in the pipeline!
You can read more about Wheelsong Books and its growing
stable of exciting new and emerging poets on the
Wheelsong Books website at: wheelsong.co.uk

Wheelsong publication list

- Ellipsis (2020) by Steve Wheeler
- Inspirations (2020) by Kenneth Wheeler
- Sacred (2020) by Steve Wheeler
- Living by Faith (2020) by Kenneth Wheeler
- Urban Voices (2020) by Steve Wheeler
- Small Lights Burning (2021) by Steve Wheeler
- My Little Eye (2021) by Steve Wheeler
- Ascent (2021) by Steve Wheeler
- Dance of the Metaphors (2021) by Rafik Romdhani
- Into the Grey (2021) by Brandon Adam Haven
- RITE (2021) by Steve Wheeler
- Absolutely Poetry Anthology 1 (2021) by various
- Absolutely Poetry Anthology 2 (2022) by various
- War Child (2022) by Steve Wheeler
- Hoyden's Trove (2022) by Jane Newberry
- Shocks and Stares (2022) by Steve Wheeler
- Autumn Shedding (2022) by Christian Ryan Pike
- Cobalt Skies (2022) by Charlene Phare
- Wheelsong Poetry Anthology 1 (2022) by various
- Rough Roads (2022) by Rafik Romdhani
- Symphoniya de Toska: Book One (2023) by Marten Hoyle
- Vapour of the Mind (2023) by Rafik Romdhani
- Nocturne (2023) by Steve Wheeler
- Symphoniya de Toska: Book Two (2023) by Marten Hoyle
- Wheelsong Poetry Anthology 2 (2023) by various
- Constellation Road (2023) by Matthew Elmore
- Beyond the Pyre (2023) by Imelda Zapata Garcia
- Symphoniya de Toska: Book Three (2023) by Marten Hoyle

All titles are available for purchase in paperback, and Kindle editions and some in hardcover on Amazon.com or direct from the publisher at: wheelsong.co.uk

Printed in Great Britain
by Amazon